GREAT EMIGRATIONS

3
The British
to Southern Africa

GREAT EMIGRATIONS

Series Editor: Douglas Hill

3
The British
to Southern Africa

Kate Caffrey

GENTRY BOOKS · LONDON

First published 1973
© Kate Caffrey Toller 1973
ISBN: 0 85614 020 1

Published by Gentry Books Limited
17 Southampton Place, London, WC1A 2EH
Designed by Brian Roll
Printed by William Clowes & Sons, Limited
London, Beccles and Colchester

To Ilsa Yardley

Every recorded fact contains the personality of the person who records it. *Frank Clements*

All sources are suspect. *A. J. P. Taylor*

The darkest thing about Africa has always been our ignorance of it. *George H. T. Kimble*

Acknowledgments

I am greatly indebted to the following people for their assistance, information, advice, and encouragement.

To C. D. Black-Hawkins, Esq., for telling me about his ancestor, Captain Hamilton Ross; to Lord Montagu of Beaulieu and his archivist, Captain H. Widnell, for allowing me access to the Montagu archives; to C. J. Brereton, Esq., for advising me about the illustrations and maps; to M. Brennan, Esq., Photographic Librarian of the Imperial War Museum; to the curators of The Mansell Collection; to Mrs Ilsa Yardley for her appreciative encouragement and indeed for making it possible for me to write this book.

There is in London at present no office of Rhodesian affairs (information on immigration must be obtained direct from Salisbury), but the Immigration Section of South Africa House, in Cockspur Street, has an exquisitely courteous and helpful staff, entirely Afrikaner, headed by the tall, distinguished Consul, Mr C. L. F. Koch of Cape Town, who generously supplied me with copies of the pamphlets and booklets beautifully compiled (by Barclays Bank among others) for the information of those intending to settle in the Union. I explained to them right away that I was not proposing to leave this country; but it made no difference: they readily afforded me every facility I asked for.

All that appears in the subsequent pages is, however, my own responsibility: those mentioned above have all my gratitude but are not to be held accountable for anything I have written.

Foreword

In writing or speaking of Southern Africa the chronicler is bedevilled at every turn by the thorny problem of names. Today's tabu is yesterday's commonplace. I have, for the sake of clarity and brevity, used words like Trekboer, Boer, Afrikaner, and African, Hottentot, Zulu, Kaffir, native, tribesman, to mean, respectively, South African of Dutch, German, or Huguenot descent, or South African of Bantu descent, in the certain knowledge that every one of these names will offend somebody: consequently in the hope that, where all are equally affronted, all will equally decide not to mind. We are all natives of somewhere and all descended from natives of somewhere.

As regards the spelling of proper names, where variations exist I have simply chosen the ones I like best.

All comments, conditions of weather, states of mind public or private, recorded in these pages, have documentary support.

I have tried throughout to avoid drawing any conclusions from the facts presented, on the basis that facts speak louder than any individual's opinion. I have left out enormous quantities of fascinating information that did not precisely fit my brief. In reading anything about Africa one finds the most incongruous details—for example, the song 'Home Sweet Home', a bobble-fringed Victorian ballad if ever there was one, was written in (of all places) Tunis. If that can happen in Africa, anything might. As I have attempted to show, however shortly, in this account, practically everything has.

Contents

Illustrations

All illustrations reproduced by permission of the Mansell Collection

Maps

Cartographer: Leo Vernon

1. A Most Stately Thing

'This Cape,' declared Sir Francis Drake in 1580, 'is a most stately thing and the fairest Cape we saw in the whole circumference of the Earth.'

Well might he say so. Others besides Drake have felt the impact of coming to this smiling territory out of the long swells off Agulhas and the swirl of great waters where the Atlantic and Indian Oceans mingle, giving the Cape of Storms its first name. Also the voyager is oppressed by the sheer mass of Africa, one-fifth of the earth's surface, still the least known continent today. As big as China, India, the United States and Europe lumped together, with its seven hundred native languages and two hundred million people, it continues to produce, as it did in the time of Pliny, always some new thing. Indeed most of it is entirely new in historical terms. Unlike North America, where apart from a few scattered Spanish missions named after (among others) Saint Francis, Saint Barbara, and Our Lady Queen of the Angels the opening up started on the east coast and pushed steadily across towards the unattainable sunset, Africa remained for centuries a fragmentary coastline only, nibbled tentatively along by various powers. It is true that in 1802 two Portuguese half-castes started out to cross it from ocean to ocean, but the journey took them nine years. No great seaways led to the interior; awesome deserts, mountains and tropical forests barred the way; it remained what to some it still is: the dark continent.

The part of Africa with which we are here concerned is the southern portion, everything south of the Zambesi. Small in comparison on the map it is still prodigious enough, almost the size of India, 1,700 miles by 1,100 at its broadest and containing six and a half countries: the African states of Botswana, Lesotho and Swaziland, half of Portuguese

1

Mozambique, the mandated territory of South-West Africa, and the republics of Rhodesia and the Union. The weight of history, the movement of British immigration, the tangle of debate and the complexity of emotional problems all deepen as one moves through this list in this order. The pattern was set from the beginning and was largely dictated by geography.

In shape compared by Mr John Cope with 'a cluster of swarming bees hanging from a branch in a mimosa tree and pushed a little to one side by the wind', Southern Africa presents a huge plateau bordered on south and east by gradually lowering chains of mountains. Half the area is desert or semi-desert. Quick-drying summer rains fret the cultivable parts with erosion. Miles of rolling grassland stretch between the lush swampy bush of the east and the sunbaked emptiness of the west. The long rivers are shallow, with sandbars, rapids, and an unnerving tendency to dry up in places, and there is no great interior lake. The perfect natural harbours on the east remained malarial and fly-ridden, on the west backed by a strip that justifiably gave it the sinister name of the Skeleton Coast. The south, how-ever, had a Mediterranean littoral that made it one of the most delectable of places. It was from the south inevitably, and overland, that the colonists moved.

The Portuguese got there first—Bartholomew Diaz with two caravels at Mossel Bay in February 1488; Vasco da Gama, naming Natal on Christmas Day, en route to India in 1497, followed by Antonio da Saldanha who discovered Table Bay and climbed Table Mountain; Francisco d'Almeida, retiring Viceroy of the Indies, calling at Table Bay on the way home in 1510—each of these had a scuffle of sorts with the local tribesmen, called Hottentots, and D'Almeida was killed. The Portuguese preferred to refresh at Saint Helena, partly because of these incidents and partly because of the dangerous tides, so they left the Cape alone. It impressed them, though, for Camões nearly a century later evoked in the *Lusiad* the great spirit, prophesying ven-geance, of the Cape of Storms. As Mr C. E. Carrington put it, 'The prize lay there for any man's possession.'

Apart from Drake, the next visitors were the Dutch, who in 1602 formed the United Chartered East India Company, that Mr Arthur Keppel-Jones called 'the world's first joint stock company on the grand scale'. From then on both

Dutch and English ships began to make landfall at Table Bay out and back on the six-month-long voyages between Europe and the Indies, leaving letters under stones for the next crew to find; one such reads: 'The *London* arived the 10 of M here from Surat bound for England and depar the 20 dicto 1622 Richard Blyth Captane. Heare under looke for letters'. Some of these stones happened to be put where today stands the General Post Office of Cape Town.

Hippo lived in the marshes of the Cape flats and lions on the slopes of Table Mountain when the first scheme of joint occupation by British and Dutch of the territory round the Cape was proposed, but after the 1623 Dutch massacre of the British at Amboina it was quietly dropped. In 1647 the *Haarlem*, an East Indiaman, was wrecked in Table Bay; without loss of life the crew did a Robinson Crusoe, camping at Green Point with their salvaged cargo that obligingly included vegetable seeds and garden tools. They planted the seeds and bartered with the Hottentots for cattle and sheep; news of this colony, carried back to Holland on subsequent ships, caused the Dutch Government to send out an expedition in 1652 (twenty-six years after setting up a similar foothold called New Amsterdam on the shores of America), when on 6 April a ship's surgeon named Jan van Riebeeck landed to found 'a refreshment station'. Like Columbus, he had sailed with three ships: the *Drommedaris* of 200 tons, the *Reijger*, much smaller, and a 40-ton yacht appropriately called *Goede Hoop*.

Van Riebeeck's party, all Company employees, planted more vegetables, bartered more livestock, built an earth fort against the Hottentots, and supplied food and medical care to Company ships, about twenty-five of which called every year. They had thirteen and a half acres of land apiece, tax free, on which they promised to live for twenty years, but they were not free to trade, nor to grow tobacco, both Company monopolies. Eventually they imported slaves from the Guinea coast and from Malaya, and, with a presage of the future, built a large hedge to keep the natives out. In 1662 when van Riebeeck relinquished his command the colony's population was 1,394, of whom thirty-six were free burghers who had come with their families. In 1688 two hundred Huguenots arrived, with names like de Villiers, Marais, de la Rey, Joubert, Malan, and brought the grape to the Cape.

They settled mainly in the Drakenstein Valley, centred

on the area of Paarl, and approved by Simon van der Stel who, becoming Governor in 1679, had planted thirty families with a minister and a teacher in the fertile valley he called Stellenbosch, following the Company policy of admitting suitable Protestants. All were well established by 1699 when van der Stel retired to Constantia, the fine white house on Table Mountain which still stands among his oak trees and vineyards. Settlers and slaves interbred vigorously, producing the first members of the community known today as Cape Coloured.

Many shipwrecks took place off the coastal strip of Natal, but ships kept on coming to Port Natal, their few survivors leaving little trace apart from a note and a legend. The note, logged in the year it was written, stated: 'Here lived in Anno 1718, a penitent Pirate, who sequestered himself from his abominable Community and retired out of Harm's Way'. The legend, repeated among the tribesmen and recorded by Mr Donald R. Morris, was of a white race dwelling on the bottom of the sea, collecting beads, and from time to time 'riding to the shore on animals with great white wings in search of the ivory on which it fed'.

During the eighteenth century the number of ships calling every year at Table Bay multiplied by six and the stone castle of Cape Town was built in jerks of construction reflecting the ups and downs of British–Dutch–French relations. Meanwhile the Dutch were settling seriously, pushing into the dry interior with their ox-wagons and staking out huge farms demarcated by the simple expedient of starting from a spring and walking a horse for half an hour in each compass direction, the result extending over six thousand acres. Most of them required two such farms, one for summer and one for winter. During the eighteenth century they had it all to themselves.

The land had no roads, no bridges, and was penetrated at the pace of the ox, to which it was suggested a monument ought to be put up for its importance in opening up the country. Because the wagons broke up the topsoil the custom developed of following in parallel, so the trek tracks were five or ten miles broad, drawing together at passes and fords, to cross which the unnailed wagons could be taken to pieces. Eighteen feet by six, covered with heavy doubled canvas, creaking along on huge wheels bound with half-inch thick iron bands, carrying a ton of household goods

4

crammed inside with the women and children, and pulled by full spans of fourteen to eighteen matched red-and-white or black-and-white oxen, yoked in pairs with the strongest pair on the düsselboom and the most experienced pair leading, the wagons moved out in search of the promised land. With amazing patience and courage, ignorant of the country and its dangers, the trekboers travelled anything from one to ten miles a day, buoyed up by their evangelistic faith and their angry Puritan bravery.

In the apparently endless silent land, isolated from the world in the age of Voltaire, Rousseau, Tom Paine, Adam Smith, Kant, Schiller, Watt, Volta, Gibbon, Johnson, Blake and Burns, their character developed. Hard, brave, stubborn and tenacious, for ever moving out of sight of their neighbour's smoke, clinging to the Old Testament and the rifle, self-enclosed and self-reliant, they simplified everything down to the basic, including their native language. They were not a frontier society like that of the Old West: that came later. Indeed they were scarcely a society at all. They pulled the frontier along with them, and their movement, echoing the coast without touching it, pressed inexorably always inland. As soon as a law or a neighbour touched them, they moved on. Their way of life, described by Mr Christopher Martin, stayed in the seventeenth century— simple houses, often dirt-floored, homespun clothes in which many slept 'ready to turn out with musket and cutlass to fight the marauding bands of Africans as had their fathers', threshing and winnowing by hand, persisted, like their practice of keeping money in chests or buried in the ground and of morning and evening Bible readings by the family patriarch. Many old Boers 'kept the lumber for their coffins cut and ready next to their beds'. The Dutch who stayed in Cape Town were as cosmopolitan as anyone, but in the end it was the trekboer who set his stamp for ever on the country.

The French and English raced for the Cape in 1780, two rival squadrons speeding south through the Atlantic and clashing briefly at Porto Praya in the Cape Verde Islands from which the French Admiral Suffren got away some hours ahead and landed in Simon's Bay. For three years the French made Cape Town a little Paris, constructing elegant buildings that have left a flavour to this day, and, spending freely, gave the Cape a short period of light-headed prosperity. They left the Cape to the Dutch in 1784, but on the

French invasion of Holland after the Revolution the Prince of Orange fled to England and authorized a British force to go to Simon's Bay and hold the Cape until he returned to power. The British under General Craig promptly took over, when in 1795 Captain Hamilton Ross of the Scots Greys hoisted the Union Jack in Cape Town and barred the way to India against France. Sir George Yonge, the British Governor, said bitterly in 1800: 'I know very well this has been presented to us as a useless Colony, and even a heavy burden, and a place not worth retaining. The assertion is false and I assert that whoever has the Cape is Master of the Commerce of India.' By the Peace of 1802 the Cape was handed back to the Dutch-Jacobin Batavian Republic maintained in Holland by French money and arms; the takeover was untidy: the *Imogene* frigate, arriving early at the Cape on New Year's day 1803, found that:

> the fortresses would have been delivered up to the Dutch in the course of a few hours; part of the English troops were embarked, and others encamped at the distance of eight miles. In consequence of the *Imogene*'s dispatches, the troops were immediately disembarked, and re-garrisoned the forts. The place was saved by about five hours. There were only about fifty men in the castle, as a matter of form, to keep possession till the Dutch entered.

But by October:

> Private letters state the Colony to be rapidly declining. The troops are constantly showing a disposition to mutiny, on account of their little pay and short allowances, which were to be equal to those given to the English garrison. The Government is also in arrears, and has neither money nor credit; and the disaffection among the garrison, which consists of 2,000 troops, is so great, that it is believed they would surrender if a British fleet were to appear off the Cape.

The Dutch-Jacobin Government alarmed the settlers by announcing a programme of administrative reforms promising secular education and religious equality, but continued to run into trouble. In 1805, Trafalgar year, Mr J. H. Tuckey, first lieutenant of the *Calcutta*, wrote:

6

*The first annexation: hoisting the British flag at Cape Colony, 1795
(from a painting by Caton Woodville)*

The English, during the short time they were masters of the Cape, raised the price of every consumable commodity 200*L.* per cent.; but the Dutch government are again endeavouring to reduce things to their former level, and, by the strictest œconomy, make the colony pay its expences. These measures are exceedingly unpopular, and have already caused upwards of 100 real or fictitious bankruptcies. Hence the partiality with which the English are viewed here. Their return is openly wished for, even by those who were formerly their greatest foes. In fact, the Dutch government at the Cape, as well as at home, is entirely under French influence; and it is probable that, in the boundless ambition of the Corsican usurper, he considers the Cape of Good Hope as one of the steps by which he intends to mount the Asiatic throne.

After this charming comment Mr Tuckey goes on to admire Cape Town, 'one of the handsomest colonial towns in the world':

The streets, which are wide and perfectly straight, are kept in the highest order, and planted with rows of oaks and firs. The houses are built in a style of very superior elegance, and inside are in the cleanest and most regular order. They are not, however, sufficiently ventilated to dissipate the stale fume of tobacco, which is peculiarly offensive to a stranger. The play-house is a neat building, erected by the English, where French and Dutch plays are acted alternately, twice a week, by private performers. The public garden, in which was a menagerie well stocked with all the curious animals of Africa, was entirely neglected by the English. Within the garden is the government-house, a neat, convenient building, in the old Dutch taste.

Run by the Governor, the Council of Policy, the Council of Justice, and the Burgher Council, all overshadowed by the Company and the Dutch Government behind that, Cape Town was a place stiff with precedence and bristling with laws about such apparently small matters as the length of a lady's train, the cost of a bridal bed, the use of umbrellas and the hours of bakers' delivery. Smoking in the street was prohibited, lest the thatched houses caught fire; watchmen walked in pairs, known as the Rattle Watch from the rattles they carried and sounded every hour; nightly there was dancing in private houses and drinking in public taverns, and the risk of falling on the homeward journey into holes in the unpaved roads. Lady Anne Barnard, the Government Secretary's wife, drank Cape wine in preference to French, made her own candles and syrup, sent Henry Dundas, Secretary of State of War and the Colonies, a box of ostrich eggs with instructions on how to cook them, and travelled throughout the habitable country. She wrote: 'Here is a divine climate, no fog, no damp . . . full of health and exhilaration to the spirits.'

But Cape Town was still a charming oasis in the wilds: in January 1806 ('upon the Capitulation of the Town and Garrison to Sir Home Popham') General Baird reported bluntly to London:

> It is my duty to inform your Lordship, that the nature of the country—a deep, heavy, and hard land, covered with shrubs, and scarcely pervious to light bodies of infantry; and, above all, the total privation of water under the effects of a burning sun, had nearly exhausted our gallant fellows.

By then some 15,000 emigrants had settled in the Cape and Natal, most of them Dutch, and most with no idea that Africa was no longer endless: in the race 'with a continent for a prize' the two folk movements, built around cattle and moving at cattle pace, brushed at the Great Fish River: the Boers pressing north, the Zulu pressing south. Cattle raids and small skirmishes crackled along the borders. The first hard news came in 1807 when the Acting Governor of Cape Colony, Du Pré Alexander, Earl of Caledon, sent a military surgeon named Robert Cowan to find his way to Delagoa Bay. Cowan took with him Lieutenant Donovan, a Griqua guide, twenty Hottentots of the Cape Regiment, and two wagons. Most of them died on the way, but not before Cowan had spent some months with a native chieftain called Dingiswayo (The Troubled One) who absorbed Cowan's ideas of tribal amalgamation and liberal rule and who later built up the nucleus of the Zulu nation.

An obscure clan chieftain named Zulu (The Heavens) was

Storming of the Cape of Good Hope, 1806

an ancestor of Chaka, born about 1787 when the clan numbered some fifteen hundred. Called up into Dingiswayo's army at the age of twenty-three, Chaka became chieftain in 1816 and developed the magnificent fighting Zulu impi that within three years had forged his nation into something no tribe in black Africa dared oppose. His kraal on the Tugela River had an interesting name: 'At the Place of He who Kills—with Afflictions'—kwa-Bulawayo. The afflictions were plentiful: when the Boers later trekked north of the Drakensberg they found vast stretches of land where skeletons outnumbered living beings.

In January 1810 one Captain Donovan of the 32nd with a surgeon and some Hottentot soldiers arrived safely in Mozambique after an eighteen-month journey from the Cape, during which, *The Gentleman's Magazine* of January 1810 rather unkindly reported:

> they had not discovered any real savages, except the Dutch inhabitants of the frontier provinces of the colony. Everywhere else they were received with kindness; they have found wild camels and cameleopards and have observed very singular arrangements in the establishments of the natives, their property, the furnishing of their houses, and the system of slavery which exists throughout the interior of Africa.

But the frontier clashes went on, armed skirmishes mounted by both Boer and Zulu along the Natal border and the Fish River. At the same time the Hottentot farm and domestic workers towards the north were breaking loose; the Government set up a pass system and circuit courts to investigate complaints, one such court being the notorious Black Circuit of 1811. Matters boiled up to the armed rebellion of 1814 led by two brothers called Bezuidenhout who were killed in scuffles after which five of their sixty followers were hanged at Slagter's Nek; in Afrikaner mythology Bezuidenhout's soul apparently goes marching on, like that of John Brown.

The Slagter's Nek decision was part of the policy of the new Cape Governor, Lord Charles Somerset, an overbearing dominator aged forty-eight who quarrelled with all his subordinates, anticipated his huge salary of ten thousand a year and disliked missionaries and intellectuals alike, but who gave the colony its eventual shape. Hopeful reports were printed in England that the early missionaries had 'met with a joyful reception in Kaffraria', but Lord Charles, surveying his territory with the hard eye of a man whose family commanded twenty-two votes in the House of Commons, realized that the new possession needed a nucleus of British settlers to stabilize it, and demanded suitable action from Whitehall.

Already a handful of British had settled in the colony, whether or not they realized it at the time. The first of them all, according to Mr John Bond, was Robert Hart, who ran away from home in Glasgow to enlist at the age of seventeen and went in 1795, a year later, to the Cape with the Argylls under General Clarke to assist General Craig. Quartered for seven years in Cape Town Castle, Hart and the rest made expeditions into the interior which they liked ('hoping to kill a unicorn for scientific Mr Barrow'), and finding only five small villages in existence: Stellenbosch, Swellendam, Paarl, Tulbagh and the 'nest of Jacobins and French principles', Graaff Reinet, a single dusty goat-strewn street edged with 'mud-huts for a dozen artisans, with a bigger mud-hut for the landdrost at the top and a tumbledown government office, also of mud, alongside'; compared with this, Scotland's poorest village seemed 'palatial'. Here in 1799 Hart's company put down a rising led by two Dutchmen, van Jaarsveld and Prinsloo (another name that was to cast shadows). The rebels were captured in a lovely area that later became Somerset East. There were Kaffir skirmishes, for which the troops had green uniforms and brown-painted gun barrels for camouflage. Hart went on to India and back to England, where in 1804 he married Hannah Tamplin of Guernsey, but by early 1807 he came back with her to Cape Town, and fought, now as a lieutenant, in the Kaffir War of 1811.

The Lieutenant-Colonel in that war was John Graham, another professional soldier, who on arrival five years before had written gaily home: 'Fancy me a black chief!' after leading his infantry ashore under fire and heading the advance on Cape Town. Officer Commanding the Cape Regiment, in which Hart served, Graham and his force were 'destined to accomplish what all former attempts, both coercive and friendly, had failed in, viz. the expulsion of the Kaffre hordes from the most fertile part of the Settlement'; the force numbered 640 regulars and had 'drained the garri-

sons' of Graaf Reinet, Algoa Bay and the Cape. Their
cavalry was supplemented by Boer commandos of whom
Graham wrote: 'I never in my life saw more orderly, willing
and obedient men . . . whenever they have been engaged
they have behaved with much spirit'. The war was won,
Graham persuaded the Boers to return home, and to protect
them he planned a system of forts along the Great Fish
River from the sea to an inland post he called after Lieutenant-General Sir John Cradock who had given him his
command. At the centre of the system was Lucas Meyer's
deserted farm, where the house, in ruins, became the officers'
mess, Graham hanging his sword on a mimosa tree at the
door. Cradock called the place Graham's Town, and Hart
was one of the first to build a house there. With his glowing
prospects Graham could now afford to marry, and chose
Johanna Catherina Cloete, a descendant of one of van Riebeeck's burghers. By the time of Waterloo, Graham was
Commandant at Simon's Town.

Others came out after Waterloo: George Thompson Bor-
radaile, one of several merchants anxious to develop trade;
Lieutenant Benjamin Moodie who went successfully with
three hundred Scottish artisans to the Cape; Robert God-
lonton, pioneer journalist; John Centlivres Chase who became the settlers' historian; and Andrew Geddes Bain, a
blue-eyed, red-haired Scot aged nineteen, who began to
trade in ivory at Graaff Reinet. Already settled at the Cape
by then was Eliza Humphrys from Chester, married to a
French Swiss musician, Louis Balthasar Meurant, emigrating in 1808 after the birth of their daughter Louisa; Meurant composed light opera for the Cape Theatre, and in June
1811 their son Louis was born. In the early twenties son and
daughter took part in the first English play produced by the
colonists (Foote's comedy The Liar); and Louis was the man
who first set down Afrikaans on paper.

But the vast wild distances with no schooling in them
brought out the missionaries. Comments sent home rever-
berated round church and state circles: William Burchell in
1811 worried how fast isolated immigrants on the frontier
lost 'the advanced civilisation of Europe'; the remedy was
an influx of Britons 'numerous enough to form an English
community and preserve their own customs'. The scientific
Mr Barrow (later Sir John) wrote ironically: 'Such is the
nature of an African boor, that having nothing in particular

to engage his attention he is glad of an excuse to ride to the distance of eight or ten days, whether it be to a church or to a vendue, to hunt elephants or to plunder the Kaffirs'. Two outstanding missionaries were already in the field: William Anderson and James Archbell. Anderson set out in a new wagon from Cape Town on 10 February 1801 to start a Griqua mission on behalf of the London Missionary Society. He started at Aat Kaap where he planted the first wheat ever sown north of the Orange, persisted for four years despite drought and smallpox, and his wife and nine children formed the first white family in the future Free State. Settled at Klaar Water, they gave hospitality to Cowan and Donovan, succoured Robert Moffat and escorted him to Kuruman, defended the Griqua against conscription, and resisted the combined threats of the authorities and of an outlaw freebooter called Coenraad du Buys. Lord Charles put on the pressure and Anderson withdrew in March 1820 to another mission at Pacaltsdorp.

The Reverend James Archbell married Elizabeth Haigh in the parish church at Leeds in 1818 and at once set out for the Cape. They opened a mission station at Rietfontein where their first child was born in an isolated hut on the veld with only the husband to assist his wife. Later they tried South-West Africa, narrowly escaping death by both thirst and drowning, and when native wars came withdrew to the Cape, where the elder daughter saw bread for the first time and refused to eat it, thinking it was soap. By 1825 the Archbells were settled at Maquassi in the future Transvaal, where Archbell published a school-book, the first book ever produced in those parts.

A gentleman from Newcastle signing himself 'G.A.' wrote on 8 January 1820 complaining that the Government had done nothing to promote knowledge of South Africa 'although we have now had it in our possession for nearly twenty years', and summed up contemporary information from travellers' reports, which

> are of no further information than to say, that it is a most extensive country, inhabited literally by nothing else than wild beasts, save here and there a few Dutch Boors; that the climate is capable of producing *Wine, Wheat, and all the Necessaries of Life*; that there are great tracts of country called *Karroo*, that produce

nothing, and are perfectly sterile; and that they lie North of the coast from Algoa Bay, or end of Seldanah Bay, by the Cragee River, or near to the Drakensleen; and get wandering away to *Graaff Rennett*, as if it was at hand, or as near to the Cape Town, as Windsor or Oxford are near to the capital of England.... The first thing that should have been set out with, as a temptation to those who might wish to emigrate there, should have been the publishing of a large Map of each division of that extensive country, for the information of those who had ideas of going there. This Map should have been done by our own Engineers: it would have been of double use, not only in making us acquainted perfectly with the boundaries of the course of the rivers, but we should have been generally informed, as to its geological productions, where the valuable mines lie, their possibility of being brought down to the coast and conveyed to Great Britain . . .

He concluded that Oxford and Cambridge should send some of their 'learned travelling fellows' out there.

This produced a reply from Mr T.W., writing from Lloyd's on 5 February, stating that he had explored parts of the Cape and agreed with Mr G.A. He set out his ideas about the quality of emigrant to look for:

Mere speculation and dash will not do, but a strong discrimination is necessary. Persons offering themselves, require to be convinced of the propriety or impropriety of *their* views; take, for instance, a poor, weak, indulged, dram-drinking weaver from his garret, put an axe or saw in his hand, or a spade and a hoe, with his blanket to sleep on, and send him to clear a spot that civilised man never before attempted, and the *creature* sinks under it; take any other indulged person, brought up in a manufactory, who wishes to emigrate with his wife and two children, so helpless as to require their food to be brought to them, and what can they do? . . . Compare this description with the restless back-woodsman in America, who, with a horse carrying all his furniture, and a wife and child, or two, perhaps, has to raise his log-house, cut down trees in a forest *as old as the creation*, clear the land, raise his Indian corn, and presently become an easy settler. If we wish to settle the Cape, it must be with such characters as these, the hardy agriculturist, not the puny manfacturer ... we shall act well, if we form a permanent and inclusive settlement in the South of Africa, for a day will come when we shall want it.

This is probably the T. Walters who wrote from Lloyd's on 29 May 1822 begging that Africa should be explored ('What is there not to be obtained by British seamen and British merchants?') and on 17 July that 'the Cape cannot be too attentively settled'. His blueprint certainly fitted the Boers, whether he ever realized it or not.

Comments such as these helped to push the government in the way Lord Charles Somerset believed it should go. The main lever that moved them was post-war unemployment, which exercised Whitehall after 1815, not for the last time. By July 1819 proposals had been drawn up and fifty thousand pounds voted through Parliament to assist passages to Southern Africa. Those wishing to go had to apply to the Secretary of State, each head of a family putting down a ten-pound deposit which would be paid back to him in tools and rations in the Colony; the first to apply from any town or village was appointed head of a party and given authority to select other suitable settlers from his own place; no party of fewer than ten would be accepted. *The Times* in support weighed in with a lyrical comment on 'our noble station at the Cape of Good Hope which has the finest soil and climate in the world'. Meanwhile a patchwork of surveying (Mr G.A. notwithstanding) was going on: in November 1817 'letters and papers from the Cape of Good Hope' reported probes eastwards along the coast 'where extensive districts produce the finest wheat'.

> So flattering are future prospects that about three hundred emigrants had lately arrived at the Cape from the Northern parts of England, to take the management and direction of the existing agricultural districts. HM Ship *Dispatch*, commanded by Sir Jahleel Brereton, had been sent by the Government to open the navigation of the river, to complete the surveys, to fix upon a harbour, and found the new Colony.—Sir Jahleel Brereton had ascertained, that there is a good

harbour in the Knysna, on the East coast of Cape Town.

In March 1818 an archaeological report came in: 'about twenty miles north of Cape Town'—

> some persons, in digging, happened to strike upon what appeared to be a beam of timber; but, tracing it, they found a ship, or other large vessel, deeply imbedded in the soil. A plank of it has accompanied the account of the discovery. It appears to be cedar, and is in a state of good preservation.

In December 1819 came a reference to the Governor:

> Captain Taylor, by the *Hottentot,* arrived in fifty-nine days from the Cape of Good Hope, intelligence has been received of total defeat of the Kaffre forces, and of the capture and defeat of the principal leaders. The *Hottentot* landed despatches for the Government at Dover. On the day before she sailed, the Governor [Lord Charles Somerset] and suite embarked on board HM brig *Redwing,* for Algoa Bay; for the purpose, as it is supposed, of making terms of peace with the savages, and fixing the future boundary of their country in the direction of the colony.

Nobody mentioned the local currency, a coin-collector's dream and a trader's nightmare, including, according to Mr C. W. de Kiewiet, 'gold mohurs and rupees from India, pagodas from Madras, johannas, doubloons, and dollars from Spain and her Empire, sequins from Venice, and guineas and shillings from England'. Paper currency was the poor quality, unstable and easily counterfeited Rix dollar which 'slowly collapsed' between 1806 and 1825 when the British Government 'decided to put it out of its misery . . . at 1s. 6d. in British silver'.

Ninety thousand Britons applied for the emigration scheme. Five thousand of these were accepted. The minimum number for each party was ten, and during the autumn of 1819 the applicants were sorted into fifty-six or fifty-seven groups totalling 3,487 men, women, and children, who among them had deposited about fourteen thousand pounds in cash. The smallest group contained fifteen people from Carlisle; the largest, two hundred and twenty, from Cork. Four hundred Scots applied through a Captain Grant 'not to be mixed in with any others as speak a different language'.

To transport this motley collection of (on the whole) utterly unprepared and ignorant people, armed with little but uncritical hope, twenty-four ships averaging 400 tons had been chartered in the ports of England, the majority, of course, in London, where, as if to emphasize the hardships they were leaving and the unknown terrors to which they were probably going, the Thames froze over at London Bridge: the last recorded occasion on which it did so. Ice in the river delayed the ships' departure during December, but at last the weather relented and they set out.

Twenty of the twenty-four ships rolled into one would not make up the tonnage of the *Queen Mary*. It is not difficult to picture the disagreeable details of the three months' journey to Table Bay: the small, cramped transports wallowing through the Atlantic, day after endless day, an infinitely further distance than the settlers had imagined (even as late as the end of the century soldiers embarking for the Cape were heard to wonder whether South Africa could be further away than Bristol), and without any of the upholstered comfort and delicious food that modern sea-passengers take for granted on the Union Castle Line. Some shiploads had additional troubles, as a report of August 1820 shows:

> The *John* transport has arrived at Portsmouth from the Cape of Good Hope. The *John* took out six hundred settlers for Algoa Bay, principally from Lancashire. The passengers were severely attacked with the measles on the voyage out; but from the great attention paid them, they soon recovered from its effects.

It was at Algoa Bay, a month's sailing from Table Bay, that the majority were landed, and today the 1820 Settlers' Monument dominates the waterfront of Port Elizabeth, and the 1820 Settlers' Association assists and advises immigrants throughout Southern Africa to this day. In 1820 there was simply an open beach, and here the arrivals found, in confused bewilderment, that only two thousand people were expected. A Welsh party had been landed at Caledon and an Irish party at Saldanha, but among the tents pitched on the beaches of Algoa Bay there were still too many settlers waiting for the wagons to take them to their proposed destinations in the Grahamstown area. Within a few weeks, however, the encampment was sufficiently straightened out for Thomas Pringle to describe it:

> It consists of several hundred tents, pitched in parallel rows or streets, and occupied by the middle or lower classes of the emigrants. . . . There were respectable tradesmen and jolly farmers, with every appearance of substance and snug English comfort about them. There were watermen, fishermen, and sailors from the Thames and the English seaports, with the reckless and weather-beaten look usual in persons of their professions. There were numerous groups of pale-visaged artisans and operative manufacturers from London and the large towns . . . squalid in their aspect, slovenly in their attire, and discourteous in their demeanour . . . Lastly, there were parties of pauper agricultural labourers sent out by the aid of their parishes, healthier perhaps than the class just mentioned, but not apparently happier in mind.

At least these people had a clear stretch of water and an open expanse of beach on which to land. Emigrants putting in at Port Natal with its notorious sand-bar, where captains would not risk their ships, found after what seemed a wet and interminable voyage that the vessels anchored in the roads and lowered passengers and cargo in baskets into rough lighters, which then with hatches battened down pushed ashore through the surf, many capsizing on the way, leaving the newcomers to wade ashore. For the lucky, agents of the companies that sold the passages might soon turn up with advice about how to reach the eventual place of settlement and the possibilities of renting a wagon in which to get there. Many stayed only because it was impossible to go back, dumped with their scanty and often unsuitable belongings in the middle of nowhere and left to begin hacking a home out of the bush; though the Boer farmers were unfailingly kind and helpful to many, and one party of Scots passed close to Somerset farm on their way to the remotest of the locations, guided by Major Robert Hart who showed them the way to the Baviaans River and gave them rations and their first fruit-trees. Now head of the farm, he appointed Pringle's brother John as his assistant and later took Pringle on a tour of the interior jungle-like forests, where they saw many elephants.

Some settlers did go back, some went on to Australia, some stayed at Algoa Bay and developed a thriving business in aiding and supplying later arrivals. Others did not stick to the way of life they had originally expected to follow: many were town-bred in the bone and, when the deposit money and government rations ran out, drifted to the established townships and took up trade. Many got into debt. Even those who knew enough about farming not to plant onions upside down found it hard to come to terms with utterly unfamiliar conditions. Parties were mixed, literates and illiterates, townsmen and countrymen, Saxons and Celts: they started squabbling on the journey out, on one ship the captain read the Mutiny Act and on another put two emigrants in irons, and some were unbearably irked by the regulation that no one might leave his party without written permission. Some leaders were weaker than their party members, and there was the normal proportion of ne'er-do-wells and rogues. The Government rations of meat, flour, tea, coffee, sugar, candles and soap soon exhausted the ten-pound deposits, and those who fought through to make some kind of farm found the wheat crops failed three years running. One settler, a man named Gunning, wrote to his former employer in England: 'You told me true when you said I might as well blow out my brains as come upon this expedition.'

At the moment when the 1820 settlers scrambled ashore at Algoa Bay Lord Charles Somerset was on leave in England, so his deputy, Sir Rufane Donkin, had been left in charge. Donkin, who named the camp Port Elizabeth as a tribute to his wife, issued rations, granted pasturage leases and gave the settlers sympathetic treatment. When the deposit money ran out he set the cost to the Government account. Among the newcomers were several who were to become celebrated: William Cock from Oxfordshire, who brought a party of ninety to the area between the Kowie and the Great Fish Rivers, who between 1836 and 1841 would create the first man-made harbour in South Africa by clearing the mouth of the Kowie; William Shaw, originally intended for the Army but now a Methodist minister, with his friend William Shepstone and their wives and children including Theophilus Shepstone, aged three—they got as far as Griqua Town but left there on 13 November 1823, Shaw wearing sheepskin coat and trousers and a home-made straw hat, to settle among the Kaffirs where Shaw introduced the first plough, described by the local chief as equal to ten wives—Shaw eventually became chaplain, instructor, spokesman and defender of the 1820 Settlers; Henry Hartley, aged four, whose father went to Bathurst and became an elephant hunter, his son in due course becoming an even greater one, trading in the north-west Transvaal in the forties and fifties, meeting the young German geologist Karl Mauch at Potchefstroom and with him discovering the old mines of Mashonaland in 1866, finding the first payable gold in 1868 and guiding the first party to the gold rush—his descendants still live at Thorndale, his farm near Magaliesburg.

Lord Charles Somerset came back in 1821 for his second five-year term of office and promptly disapproved of both Donkin and the settlers. Believing that cattle tempted tribal raids and wishing to keep the settlers in close communities, he cancelled the pasturage leases. Convinced that they were all 'suspect radicals' he employed agents to report on them: Mr Carrington's delightful note refers to 'agents among whom moved obscurely the mysterious figure known as "Oliver the Spy"'. Military as well as civil governor, Somerset denied the settlers civil rights, and forbade them to keep slaves, though he kept them himself and so did the Dutch burghers. The settlers began to agitate, supported by the missionaries, and their complaints reached England; starting its great liberal tradition, the first number of *The Manchester Guardian*, printed on 5 May 1821, carried an article on 'the oppression of the settlers in Cape Colony'. In 1823 a Commission, headed by Mr J. T. Bigge, went out to investigate and report back, its briefing including proposals for administrative reform, which in due course suggested the setting-up of an advisory council for the Governor, the appointment of independent judges, trial by jury, freedom of the Press, division of the Colony into two provinces, and the establishment of English as the official language. Somerset fought every inch of the way against any and all reforms, Donkin came home to attack him in the Commons, *The*

Times added its powerful voice to the colonists' cause, and in 1826 Somerset was dismissed, together with his patron, Lord Bathurst, now Secretary for War and the Colonies. Both men left places in South Africa named after them, and the fact that in their first three years the 1820 settlers managed better than the first Virginians and at least no worse than the first Dutch at Table Bay. In the period that saw the Congress of Vienna and the first moves to establish independent Belgium, the age of the Regency, the years reflected in the opening chapters of *Vanity Fair* and the novels of Jane Austen, the foothold of Britain on the southern part of Africa was fixed firmly, once and for all.

2. Mid-Century

The London Missionary Society had come fairly early into the field. In 1808 they set up a Hottentot community at Bethelsdorp near Algoa Bay, and twelve other stations scattered inland, all regarded dubiously by the Boers. But their work did not spring into fame and prominence until Dr John Philip was appointed agent in 1819. From the moment of landing in Africa he plunged into controversy, indefatigably visiting the stations, writing copious letters to William Wilberforce, Thomas Fowell Buxton, and other reformers of like persuasion so that they brought pressure to bear on the Colonial Office, conferring with tribal chiefs, discussing politics and religion, and still finding time in April 1822 to send a letter to London describing a mermaid, three feet long and hideously ugly, 'now exhibiting' in Cape Town. Protesting against the sequence of laws passed during the previous ten years that bound the Hottentots to their employers, believing that white and black should live in separate states in order to avoid exploitation of one by the other, he campaigned ceaselessly and vigorously for land to be safeguarded to the chieftains. This roused against him the natural hatred of the land-hungry trekkers, and the fruit of his work, the famous Ordinance Fifty, passed in 1828, combined with it to make him particularly detested by the white colonists. Ordinance Fifty made Hottentots and Europeans equal before the law, enabled them to buy land, abolished the pass law, ensured that children could be apprenticed only with their parents' consent, and prescribed exact limits of relationship between masters and servants. A flood of native complaints, many genuine, many not, instantly broke over the colonists' heads, provoking Anna Steenkamp's famous comment that it would be best to trek north where there was 'none of this ungodly equality', and the equally famous manifesto by her brother, the Boer leader Piet Retief: 'Whilst we will take care that no one shall be held in a state of slavery, it is our determination to maintain such regulations as may suppress crime, and ensure and preserve proper relations between master and servant'. It was not only the Dutch who objected to Ordinance Fifty: many British settlers, seeing their status threatened, felt just as strongly.

European matters naturally seemed calmer the further away one went from Cape Town. Of the mission stations the most celebrated was Kuruman, run by the nobly bearded Scot Robert Moffat, who had come out two years before Philip. In 1829 two indunas arrived at Kuruman from their tribal chief, Mzilikaze; Moffat welcomed them to his workshops, forge, and richly flowering gardens, and showed them the mysteries of his water supply. He and Archbell accompanied them back, with two wagons, setting out on 9 November. In camp on the way they were woken up by the 'frightful fury' of rhino and buffalo but made them 'fly off after receiving two or three balls'. After two weeks' travel they came to the first Matabele outpost near 'a beautiful and gigantic tree' containing seventeen conical houses built among the branches, each with enough room for one person to stand upright in the middle, on floors seven feet wide, each furnished with 'a hay carpet, a spear, a spoon, and a bowl of locusts', the topmost house some thirty feet above the ground. They passed through ruined villages where broken doorways and walls still showed ornamentation and good polished plastering, and at last reached the royal kraal, situated where Pretoria stands now.

Mzilikaze was fascinated by the moving houses, which the wagons seemed to him, and asked to see them walk, though he thought the wheels were alive, and would not cautiously approach the first wagon without clinging to Moffat's hand. He thought Moffat omniscient, did not mind Moffat's protesting against war, became embarrassingly fond of him, repeating: 'My heart is all white as milk; I am still wondering at the love of a stranger who never saw me', hated the idea of parting, rode with the party some distance back on one of the wondrous wagons and made Moffat promise to come again, which he did five times over the next thirty years.

Moffat could not help liking Mzilikaze, though he de-

scribed his rule as 'horrid despotism' and was appalled at
the number of his wives, though he wrote philosophically:
'Solomon had just as many!' He also disapproved of their
nakedness, partly on aesthetic grounds: writing to his wife
Mary he commented that:

> if fatness constitutes beauty, Mzilikaze's wives might
> come in for a share, as most of them are huge women
> with large hanging dairies and great bellies with navels
> so thoroughly surrounded with fat that a swallow with
> a little labour might make a comfortable nest in them.

The young girls wore tiny blue and white beaded aprons,
about six inches by three, which caused one of Moffat's
party to exclaim somewhat regretfully: 'It is an extraordi-
nary thing that no matter how they sat or stooped, this little
affair effectually hid what they wanted to hide'.

Among the Bechuana at that period the great terror was
the wild Mantatee horde, which cut a swath of massacre
across their territory. Undeterred by this, two missionaries,
Thomas Laidman Hodgson and Samuel Broadbent, set out
on New Year's Day 1823 to cross the Vaal river, taking with
them their wives, two young children and two English
nursemaids. They placidly brewed the first afternoon tea
ever sipped in the Transvaal and accepted shelter from the
friendly Bechuana; the eventual encounter with the Mantatee proved something of an anti-climax, for the ones they
met, terrified by houses walking on wheels, fled at the sight
of white faces staring, white arms beckoning. None the less,
survival was not easy, though Hodgsons and Broadbents
alike were utterly charmed by the beauty of the country.
On 1 July 1823 Mrs Broadbent's son was born, the first
white child born in the Transvaal. Next year Broadbent was
invalided back to Grahamstown, whereupon Hodgson threw
in his lot with Archbell.

Others were busy exploring, too, who were not missionaries. Lieutenant Francis George Farewell, a forceful man
of thirty-three from Tiverton, distinguished by widely set
slanting eyes and a long nose, had formed a trading company to open up Natal, which he set out to do early in 1824
with two ships, the sloop *Julia* and the brig *Antelope*, and
a party of twenty Boer farmers and ten English merchant-
venturers led by Henry Francis Fynn, aged twenty-one,

shrewd-eyed and open-faced but already going a bit thin on top. They crossed the sandbar of Port Natal at low tide and anchored where the custom-house stands today, pitching camp in a hollow clearing from which they were driven at midnight by a violent storm. Moving higher and relighting the fire, they then had to use firebrands to beat off wild dogs, one of which darted close enough to seize a pair of trousers; the owner, remembering that there was a sixty-dollar note in the pocket, snatched them back, at the cost of one of the legs. Next day the party camped on the future site of Durban station, took the ship's mainsail, made a tent, surrounded it with a fence of brushwood at which the dogs were content to howl at a distance, and the following morning started building a timber-framed wattle and daub house twelve feet square.

Fynn found sixty natives sheltering by the creek, so frightened of the Zulu that they hardly dared 'come out of the bush to get fish, their only sustenance' and living 'in a most distressful and famished condition'. They said Chaka lived thirty days' march to the north, which surprised Fynn, who had thought him much nearer, but all the same Fynn set out to visit the terrible monarch, taking his interpreter Frederick and two native servants, Jantyi and Mahamba, whom he called John and Michael. They were terrified by crocodiles at the Umgoni River, but got across; twelve miles further along the coast, stopping to make a fire and boil water for coffee, all three helpers bolted in a panic into the bush at the sight of a vast column of Zulu in full armed war-dress coming along the wide beach. Fynn was alarmed, but smiled weakly at them and kept repeating Chaka's name; they recognized him as a member of the bead-gathering race and passed by. Next day villagers were found, very polite, who gave Fynn one of their two cows so that he should not starve.

Fynn was asked not to go on until messengers had reported his presence to Chaka. Three days later a party arrived from the north with courteous greetings and four oxen, and escorted Fynn to their kraal, where he impressed them by curing a sick woman, something scarcely worth bothering with in the natives' opinion. With the next welcoming party came one of Chaka's senior indunas with a gift of forty head of cattle and seven elephant tusks, saying that Chaka would be glad to meet Fynn some weeks later

when his army was fully rested. Fynn went back to Fort
Natal where building was going on well enough for Farewell
to declare a holiday in July: the British ensign was hoisted,
two cannon and some muskets fired, and the Boers declared
the area was unsuited to peaceful farming, so the *Julia* took
them back to the Cape, leaving eight Englishmen and three
Africans as the founders of Natal.

Eventually an escort one hundred strong came to take
Fynn and Farewell the hundred miles to kwa-Bulawayo.
Fynn had with him ten Europeans, thirty-four natives, and
a pile of presents including every sort of bead available in
the Cape, woollen blankets, brass lacquered bars and sheets
of copper, a basket of pigeons, cats, dogs, a pig, and a full-
dress military coat with gold epaulettes. Journeying steadily
northwards they noticed the order and discipline of the
Zulu, the cleanliness of their huts, and the strings of messengers coming and going, several a day, between them and the
king. On the fourteenth day they arrived: Fynn gave a
riding display, Chaka laid on a dancing display, adored the
military coat and was fascinated by the pig, and was deeply
impressed by Fynn's curing him of stab wounds by bathing
them in camomile tea and bandaging them with linen from
the medicine chest he always carried, along with his normal
personal equipment of two blankets, a feather pillow, a
coffee-pot, and boxes of sea-biscuits and rice.

Before leaving, Fynn and Farewell saw four of Chaka's
court witness the king setting his mark to a document
granting them a tract of land round Port Natal stretching
fifty miles inland and twenty-five miles along the coast. News
of this reached London in a report from the *Baracouta* at
Port Natal,

> on the Kaffre coast, where a settlement is formed by Mr
> Farewell of the Navy; who has had a large tract of the
> country ceded to him by the King Charkee, the present
> Sovereign of the Northern part of Kaffraria. His princi-
> pal object is the collecting of ivory, and of which he
> has three tons only. A destructive war now raging in
> the country cannot but be hurtful to his views and
> success. He has about thirty natives and two Europeans
> attached to him, and is about commencing farming. We
> found him in want of some kind of provisions, with
> which he was supplied from the *Leven*.

The British to Southern Africa

The *Leven* and *Baracouta* were sister ships, engaged on surveying the coast from Delagoa Bay where in 1825 they found the inhabitants 'in as wretched a condition as can be imagined; degraded and oppressed', and where a quarrel blazed up with the Port Governor who had seized the brig *Eleanor* of London. The surveys struggled on in spite of malaria, and Captain Owen of the *Leven* found an interpreter, a local native called Shamagwava but known as English Bill to the crew; he had seven wives and five (passable) languages. Slowly they moved down the coast, where Point Durnford, Cape Vidal and Boteler Point were named after the officers who charted them. At length they regained Cape Town, where a ball was held on board, and English Bill was received by the Governor.

Reports of distress among the tiny community of Natal reached the Cape in 1825, and the brig *Mary*, James Saunder King commanding, set out on 26 August to the rescue, taking Nathaniel Isaacs, born in Canterbury in 1808, who had been working in his uncle's counting-house on Saint Helena for three years and wanted to move to a less boring locality. King brought the *Mary* up to the Port Natal sandbar on 1 October, and there she struck, becoming a waterlogged wreck from which all were saved, though one sailor had to be rescued by a Newfoundland dog.

Farewell was away on a visit to Chaka, Fynn was away exploring, so King and his crew had to manage as best they could They set to work to build another ship, while Isaacs looked around, trying a little trading and keeping a journal in which, according to Mr Morris, 'he misnamed almost every plant and animal he saw', but he knew he was seeing something unique in its way and persisted, full of the liveliest curiosity. Fynn turned up two weeks later, bearded, barefoot, and 'sunburned to the bone', and Farewell five days after that; the two took King off to present him to Chaka and left Isaacs in charge. He was called to treat a native with throat cancer, and 'did his best with chicken soup, Epsom salts, soap liniment and a red woollen bandage, and so impressed the bystanders that his patient's prompt death was not held against him'. When Farewell came back, he lent Isaacs his horse and sent him to fetch some ivory he had left in a cache near the Tugela; Isaacs made use of the trip to visit Chaka himself, the first of several such visits. The most important was in 1829, when Chaka was dead, and Fynn and Farewell were anxious to establish good relations with his successor, Dingaan, so they sent Isaacs with fifty natives and a stock of presents to make sure that their land-agreement would not become void. On 29 April Isaacs arrived, and received a good impression of Dingaan as a king 'likely to be esteemed by his subjects'.

This was not the estimate made of Dingaan by the Boers. They were already determined to trek away from the sphere of British influence, and many reasons are still given for the series of Boer movements during the eighteen-thirties: it is enough that they are folklore. The Great Trek itself began in 1837 when some 3,000 Boers converged on Thaba'nchu under various leaders: Louis Trigardt, Janse van Rensberg, Sarel Cilliers, Piet Uys, Gerrit Maritz, Hendrik Potgieter, Andries Pretorius, Piet Retief. They had to fight to get that far: brushes with the Zulu were common, culminating in Potgieter's defence of Vegkop, where the wagons were pulled into a circle or *laager* round a central group of four wagons sheltering the women and children, the gaps in the *laager* plugged with thornbush, and the Boers firing at their attackers. Often enough their wives did the reloading for them. More than a thousand wagons rolled slowly into the highveld, attracted by reports of land rich in grass and water; Potgieter led them to Potchefstroom and Retief pressed boldly on to the great escarpment of the Drakensberg, crossing into Dingaan's country. At the kraal on the Tugela the Boers obtained Dingaan's mark to a land-concession; sixty-nine of them entered the kraal while the Reverend Francis Owen, a local British missionary, drew up the document on 6 February 1838. Dingaan displayed a friendly face, but beneath it he was profoundly troubled at this invasion of his tribal territory, Chaka's legacy; finally fear triumphed. Shouting: 'Kill the wizards!' he signalled the massacre of all sixty-nine, of which Owen was the horrified witness.

Details of the massacre, set down by a Boer called Bezuidenhout who reported that the signed document had been found on Retief's body, decided the Boers to settle the account themselves. Fifty wagons led by Potgieter and Pretorius crossed into Zululand and drew up their *laager* on a bend of the Blood River, where on 16 December the Zulu attacked. Three thousand of them were killed at the price of three Boers wounded: Pretorius said that 'God made them as stubble to our sword'. Ever since then 16 December, Dingaan's Day, has been a hallowed Boer anniversary.

The trek movements continued, aiming always at the desired rate of six miles a day but not always achieving it, and not moving at all on Sundays, though they were not always sure which day of the week it was, and some turned south against the British coastal settlements. Alarmed, the Cape Governor sent 200 men of the 27th Regiment under Captain Smith to restore order; attacking the Boer camp at Congella, the British were beaten off with a quarter of their men wounded and seventeen killed. A young man, Richard King, the Paul Revere of South African history, set off to fetch help. Swimming his horse across the river, hiding by day and riding by night through six hundred miles of wild and hostile territory, he reached Grahamstown in nine days, and just over a week later the relief troops arrived by sea at Port Natal and pushed the Boers back. On 15 July 1842 the Boers submitted to the authority of the Queen in return for an amnesty, and a year later Natal became a British colony.

Now throughout the highveld from the Orange to the Vaal and beyond were some ten thousand Boer settlers. Sometimes they were loosely organized in groups that set up tiny republican communities and then split and trekked again, parties of settlers taking land where they found it, so long as it allowed them to 'subdue the heathen to honest labour' and to be free of the irksome British. The British authorities meanwhile spent some time worrying about whether these Boers came under their jurisdiction or not. Eventually they hit upon the brilliant idea that, as the Boers had carried British soil on their boots when they crossed the Orange, they remained British subjects no matter what.

All this time the steady trickle of British immigrants was percolating into the colonial territories. It was never, at any time, a flood like the great movements to America, Canada and Australia at certain periods, and, also unlike them, it did not enter a comparatively empty place. It dribbled into a land already peopled, and never from the first Briton's arrival to the present day has the number from the United Kingdom equalled the total of Afrikaners. None the less, as Mr John Bond has forcibly pointed out, it was the English-speaking South Africans who set up the rule of law and free speech, turned the tide of native invasion, founded the education system, built roads, opened harbours, created the postal, telegraph and railway services, developed banks, opened up mines, started the industrial revolution, brought in the parliamentary tradition, founded the cites, converted the heathen, and, the crowning irony, revived and expanded the Dutch Reformed Church.

One early note in *The Gentleman's Magazine* of August 1828 sketches a couple of these activities:

> Accounts from Cape Town state that King Chacka, a powerful chief, had made an attack upon several of our Chiefs, on the frontiers of the Colony. Chacka had sent some of his people as spies, who had arrived in the Colony, but the Government would not allow them to come to Cape Town.—In the new Courts of Justice, Trial by Jury, in criminal cases, had given great satisfaction.

And the indefatigable *Baracouta* found time that October to report that:

> The *Albatross*, with a large party from the ships, went up the river for the purpose of shooting some hippopotami: they suceeded in obtaining and bringing down two, but nearly with some loss; for two or three of the party straggling from the rest were attacked by an elephant, and one of the gentlemen was somewhat hurt by him.

In January 1825, Somerset East became a township, and Robert Hart retired to farm at Glen Avon nearby, where his descendants live yet. He befriended the missionaries and helped to found the local Dutch church; more surprisingly, Somerset East 'astounded the frontier' by holding an agricultural show in 1826. Already the importance of sheep was clear: by 1823 Miles Bowker and his nine sons had introduced the first Cape merino rams near Bathurst.

But one development of vital importance was the progress made in education. The 'meester' occupied a position in Southern Africa very like that of the nurse in England before Miss Nightingale got going. The educational Nightingales of the Cape arrived on the *Arethusa* on 2 July 1822: James Rose Innes of Aberdeen, a seventh child, coming out under a five-year contract for eighty pounds a year and a house; William Robertson, aged seventeen, and Andrew Murray, both going to Graaff Reinet; the Reverend John Taylor to Cradock and the Reverend George Morgan to Somerset East; the Reverend Alexander Smith going with Rose Innes to Uitenhage; Robert Blair, William Dawson, Archibald Brown, and Dr George Thom. Between them they revolutionized the concept of education in the Cape. Rose Innes married the daughter of the Cape Town Castle Governor, and in 1820 received an invitation to apply for the Chair of Mathematics at 'a South African college'. He jumped at it. London read a report in January 1830:

> The South African College opened, at the Cape of Good Hope, on 1 October last. The branches for which professors and teachers have been already provided, are—the English, Dutch, French, and classical languages; writing, arithmetic, geography, astronomy, mathematics, and mechanics. The professors are the Rev. Mr Judge, the Rev. Mr Faure, the Rev. Mr Adamson. The two latter gentlemen have offered their services gratuitously for one year, to afford time for procuring suitable persons from Europe.

Dr James Adamson, described by his employers as 'a prodigy of learning', had in fact been one of the founders of the College in June 1829, two years after his arrival at the Cape. A co-founder was John Fairbairn, thirty-five years old, a short pugnacious man with sparkling eyes and a strong Scottish accent, who married Dr Philip's daughter Eliza. Fairbairn had started a school with Thomas Pringle, and later the two of them started a newspaper, *The South African Commercial Advertiser*, which ran into trouble with Lord Charles Somerset; there ensued a three-year running battle, not the last in South Africa's history, over the censorship. Pringle wrote:

> It was difficult to conjecture to what lengths the violence of arbitrary power would at this dismal period proceed. Fear is the most cruel of all passions, and infuriated by fear or exposure, the Colonial government seemed determined to strike down every man who should dare even to look or think disapprobation of

the deeds. A frightful system of espionage pervaded
every circle of society, and rendered perilous even the
confidence of the domestic hearth. Informers and false
witnesses abounded, and rumours of plots and disloyal
combinations against the Government were assiduously
kept afloat, for purposes as obvious as they were mis-
chievous.

The paper had its ups and downs and so did the college,
its number of students at one time falling to seven, but the
combined exertions of Adamson, Fairbairn, Rose Innes,
Professor Main of Glasgow and Langham Dale, who arrived
in 1847, hauled it finally to its feet and kept it there. Rose
Innes, horrified to find that in 1839 there were only twelve
schools (which meant twelve schoolmasters) to serve an area
of 150,000 square miles, drew up the first school syllabus
in South Africa, and in 1841 paid a visit to his native Scotland, from which he returned with an LL.D. degree, seven
more schoolmasters, and five hundred pounds' worth of
maps and textbooks to start his scheme of farm schools. He
succeeded in establishing the educational system so firmly
over the next eighteen years that, a week after he died in
December 1873, another Aberdonian, the Reverend John
Brebner, crossed the Orange to do for the Free State what
Rose Innes had accomplished for the Cape Colony.

As early as May 1833 some British had crossed the Orange,
among them James Archbell and John Edwards, who found
a vast land crammed with game but empty of people, and
opened a mission station among the pale gold and blue
mountains of the eastern region. They helped the trekboers
who passed by, and Archbell was offered the job of official
chaplain to the Great Trek, but would not leave 'his people'.
He too revisited Scotland, taking two boys aged ten and
twelve from Graaff Reinet to be educated there in 1838; the
boys were John and Andrew Murray, who later became
leaders in the Dutch Reformed Church. By 1841 Archbell
was back at Griqua Town, where he started a newspaper,
The Natal Independent, and a bank for which he issued his
own banknotes. Eventually he became mayor of Pietermaritzburg, one of the first mayors in South Africa, and
found time to translate the gospels into Bantu.

In 1830 the Cape Governor was Lieutenant-General Sir
Galbraith Lowry Cole, an Irishman who had served with

that other Irish soldier, Wellington, and he had organized the building of a road across the Fransch Hoek Pass. Lady Anne Barnard had crossed the pass by a track of sorts in 1798 and found it 'very perpendicular' with its huge cliffs, and Sir Lowry was delighted with his achievement, but infuriated by the Government's suggestion that he should pay for it out of his own pocket. One of his secretaries, John Montagu, who had fought at Waterloo at the age of eighteen, was equally interested in road-building, and turned his attention to the difficult crossing of Cradock Kloof, of which an army officer reported to him in 1840:

> It is the most impossible place for horses, much less wagons, to get over I ever beheld. It is positively as perpendicular, in parts, as the face of Table Mountain. The distance is only five and a half miles but what with accidents and detentions it was nothing uncommon for a wagon to be three days getting over the barrier.

Montagu decided to use convict labour to build the road. There were about five hundred convicts in the Colony by then, scattered among the few ramshackle country jails, and he set up centres to form them into road-gangs, teaching them to read at the same time for good measure. Under Captain White the Montagu Pass was built by 1849 and opened on 19 January by the Governor; soon three mails a week were making the journey between Cape Town and Grahamstown in seventy hours, and a half-ounce letter could go anywhere in the Colony for the price of its fourpenny blue triangular stamp. Wagonmakers prospered: one in the township of George had five years' orders in advance for sprung carts and carriages. To round off his work thoroughly, Montagu created the first road board.

He had meanwhile grappled with the problem of a road across the Cape Flats, where for years the wine farmers had had to struggle across the shifting dunes with their wagons half empty because of the weight. Between 1840 and 1845 the Hard Road to Stellenbosch was constructed under the skilful supervision of Colonel Charles Michell, and, though it cost £40,000, it saved over £20,000 a year to the Colony as more than 50,000 vehicles a year used it from the moment it was open. The sand had been the problem: although the causeway ran sixteen feet above their level it still became covered with drifts in places. On the same principle as the planting of marram grass that stabilized whole stretches of the coastal sands in north Lancashire, Montagu planted the Hottentot fig and shrubs imported from Australia—wattle, willow, hakea—and the road stayed clear.

Cole's successor, Major-General Sir Benjamin D'Urban, requested a road to run from Grahamstown through the chain of forts, and Montagu appointed Andrew Geddes Bain to superintend the work of Major Selwyn's construction gangs. This was the start of eight years of brilliant work on the part of Bain: the Queen's Road, so called because it started in the year Victoria was crowned, was a seventy-mile metalled highway cut along mountainsides, spanning ravines and rivers, and Bain followed it up by building the road between Grahamstown and East London, after which Montagu put him in charge of all the road-works of the West Province. By 1 December 1848 the first fast highway from the Cape to the Orange was completed, reducing the time from twenty days to twelve between Cape Town and Beaufort West and going on through Colesberg to the Orange River. It included the spectacular Michell's Pass. Bain then took a road over the Wellington Mountains, opening Bain's Kloof in 1853: its retaining walls, over fifty feet high, still stand as a showpiece of admirable road engineering after more than a century.

The sandbar of Port Natal was still a problem. In 1849 the total revenue of Natal was only £33,000 a year, but John Milne estimated that the necessary stone pier would cost £78,000. He found the suitable stone and two immigrants to help him, Richard Godden and William Campbell (grandfather of Roy Campbell, the South African poet). Mr Bond describes how, to carry the stone across the sands to the ferry, Godden and Campbell laid the first railway track in South Africa, 'a crude tramline of hewn milkwood poles'. Somehow the pier was built, watched at every turn by Milne, who, wearing 'a long Nankeen coat and a broad Manilla hat', and nicknamed 'Old Mortality', seemed 'as imperishable as his stone pier'.

But the railways in earnest had to come. The guiding spirit behind these was John Molteno, who came to the Cape in 1831 aged seventeen to work in the South Africa Library. By 1837 he had left the Library and established an export firm; then he went into farming near Beaufort West where he opened a bank. After his wife and child died in 1843 he started planning the railway system. To reduce costs he reduced the projected gauge from four feet eight and a half inches to three feet six, and the 'Cape gauge', as it became known, was thenceforward the standard for Africa. To assist him came William Brounger, who had built railways in Denmark and put up the Crystal Palace in London before emigrating in 1858 as railway engineer of the Cape Town railway and Dock Company. By European standards the new lines had awesome gradients: one in forty in Cape Colony, one in thirty in Natal. A certain John Nixon visited the Hex River section while it was building, staying for a while in a hut with a primitive kind of air-conditioning: the corrugated iron roof was thickly covered with bushes and the windows had coconut fibre frames with streams of water trickling down them; the resident genius had brought a punkah from India and fixed it up in his living-room. But the camp at the summit of the pass was not so luxurious: Nixon slept in

> a canteen of corrugated iron sheets thrown rather than built together. My bedroom, which had no door, opened on to the bar, which was filled with Natives of all colours in various stages of drunkenness who made the night hideous with their songs and quarrels. My bed was a truckle bed in empty brandy cases, filthy to a degree. Luckily I always carry Keatings.

So, piece by piece, the land was opened up; little clusters of make-do huts grew into small towns, each with its church or school or both, and the roads and railways crept out, east and north, across the fair but challenging face of the continent. In 1849 one John Byrne approached the Secretary of State for the Colonies, Earl Grey, with a plan for settlement in Natal; after some correspondence with Governor Smith this was approved, and on 1 October the first batch of immigrants landed. Byrne bought land on the Illovo River by the following May through his agent, John Moreland, at four shillings an acre, and a village was laid out. As the settlers there came from the Montagu estates the village was originally called Beaulieu, later changed to Richmond after an estate owned by Walter Francis, fifth Duke of Buccleuch, and the immigrants, including Samuel Strapp who opened an inn and Joseph and Charles Dacomb who set up the general store, were referred to as 'the Duke's people'. The first schoolmaster of Richmond was William McKenzie of Edinburgh, who sailed with his wife and two children in *The Conquering Hero* in 1850. On arrival they had no house, so they resourcefully covered a four-poster bed with a tarpaulin and lived under that until a house was built for them. Richmond, where the principal street was called Shepstone Street, had an Old West flavour for a while, situated as it was on 'the gun-running road' whereby arms were smuggled up into Pondoland for use in the native skirmishes. In the Duke's estate accounts at Beaulieu, exquisitely written in copperplate now faded to a delicate pale brown, appears the following, headed '1850 Emigration Expences':

Feb^{ry} 1	John Godden Expences to London to see his Friends before going to Natal	£1	0	0
4	Henry Pocock Expences to London to make arrangements respecting the Emigrants	£2	2	0
8	Messrs Scammell and Company for Ironmongery	£1	15	10
	M. Huntsman for Tools	£1	1	3
21 to 25	Expences taking Emigrants to Portsmouth, putting them on board the 'Lady Bruce' to take them to Port Natal	£8	19	2
	Edward Collins Hire of Vessel for taking the Emigrants to Portsmouth and putting them on board the 'Lady Bruce'	£3	0	0
Decr 23	Benjamin Edgington for Tents for the Emigrants upon their arrival at Natal	£27	2	2
	Total	£45	0	5

John Robert Dunn, son of a drunken 1820 settler who was trampled to death by an elephant when John was fourteen,

Bay and settlement of D'Urban, 1850

and whose mother died four years later, leaving him on his own with nothing to help him but a knowledge of Zulu and great skill with a rifle, became assistant Border Agent to Captain Joshua Walmsley on the Tugela and later a white chief under the Zulu king's paramount authority, settling in Zululand for good in 1856; James Rorke, whose father had landed with his Irish regiment at Mossel Bay in 1821 and stayed on, came in 1849 to the Buffalo River where he farmed 3,000 acres and built a thatched house of stones and homemade bricks; it had eleven rooms, five of which opened only on the outside, as he disliked inside doors. Ten miles away rose the mountains, one of which had a shape that caught the eye: it was known as Isandhlwana. The farmer made a ford across the Buffalo close by his farm, and the traders, hunters and natives who used it referred to it as Rorke's Drift. The thunderclap of Blood River had sent Mzilikaze to find a fresh home far to the north, among the Matabele, but he named his new kraal after the old one, kwa-Bulawayo, and it is there to this day. Moffat visited him there in 1854, but by then a new and eminent explorer had arrived in Africa: David Livingstone.

Livingstone, a Scot of humble origin like Moffat, and like him a member of the London Missionary Society, achieved two great things: he explored as far north as the Zambesi, which he believed was 'God's highway' to the interior, and where he discovered 'the smoke that thunders' and renamed it the Victoria Falls; and he set in motion the subsequent missions that were to open up all Africa. In a speech at Cambridge in 1857 he made his legacy clear:

> I direct your attention to Africa. I know in a few years I shall be cut off in that country, which is now open. Do not let it be shut again. I go back to Africa to try to make an open path for commerce and Christianity. Do you carry out the work I have started.

Livingstone, who found the source of the Congo when he had been looking for the source of the Nile, who tried to stop the slave trade in the interior and left it flourishing more than ever, whose meeting with Henry Stanley in 1871 is the one incident everybody remembers because Stanley was so nervous that he greeted Livingstone with formality, and who was buried in Westminster Abbey, triumphed, as many have done before and after him, in death rather than in life. Among other things he had travelled nearly thirty thousand miles in Africa, discovering six lakes and the biggest waterfall in the world, and adding a million square miles to the map, but it was his work that finally got the slave trade in Africa wiped out. He was Moffat's son-in-law, too, so perhaps some of his vast credit may reflect on Moffat.

Moffat sent his son and daughter-in-law, John Smith and Emily Moffat, to set up a Matabele mission, and Mzilikaze paid them a visit. Emily wrote:

> He eyed everything eagerly, and is not above begging for anything he fancies. There were some wild flowers on the table in a mug, and he asked if they were to be 'eaten'! His Majesty wore a cap, great-coat, and a few beads round his ankles.

Not all the missionaries were encouraged by their local chieftains. A Scottish missionary, F. S. Arnot, was told by the Basuto chief Lewanika: 'Yes, yes, that is good, to read, write, and to know numbers. But don't, don't teach them the Word of God; it's not nice. No, no, you must not teach that in this country.'

The coast from time to time still took its toll: not for nothing was it believed haunted by the spectral ship, the *Flying Dutchman*. In 1852, between Cape Town and Port Elizabeth, the troopship *Birkenhead* struck a reef and sank. In order to hold the ship level while the civilians took to the boats, the 506 soldiers on board, mostly young recruits, were paraded on the quarter-deck and stood in their ranks, where they stayed until the ship went down, 357 of them being drowned. This piece of heroism sent a frisson of admiring horror throughout the world; the King of Prussia ordered the story to be read out on parade to every regiment of the army.

But there was an occasional lighter touch, too: in 1858 the Reverend Canon George Ogilvie from Calne in Wiltshire arrived at the Cape to become Precentor of Saint George's Cathedral and Headmaster of Saint George's Grammar School. Educated at Winchester and Wadham, thirty-two years old and described by the Archbishop of Cape Town as 'a strong, manly Christian', he introduced the Cape to a form of football known then as the Winchester Code.

It was a combination of soccer and rugby, played with a large round ball on pitches 150 yards long, and Ogilvie thought it would provide young Cape Town businessmen with 'a healthy form of winter exercise'. Mr A. C. Parker says that matches took place between teams calling themselves Town v Suburbs, Civil Servants v All Comers, Home v Colonial Born, and on 23 August 1862 the *Cape Argus* reported a Military v Civilians match on Green Point Common, kicked-off by Adriaan van der Byl. The players included John X. Merriman, a future Prime Minister of Cape Colony, and the spectators included Philip Wodehouse, the Governor, and his wife. The match was abandoned after an hour and three-quarters because the wind changed and 'this would have given the Military an unfair advantage which they were far too sporting to accept'. The score was 0–0. Whether anyone knew it or not, rugby football, the sporting glory of South Africa, had arrived.

Of all the Cape Governors, the most colourful was Harry George Wakelyn Smith of the Rifle Brigade, appointed on 1 December 1847 at the age of fifty and chosen by the British Army historian as the pre-eminent fighting soldier of his generation. A tough, wiry, dark-faced man of inexhaustible vitality and restless charm, he had fought through the Peninsular War, at Waterloo, served in America and India. At Badajoz he had rescued, and at once married, a young Spanish girl of lively personality, Juana de Léon, who accompanied him on his subsequent campaigns. It was after her that the South African town of Ladysmith was named. It was Harry Smith who, in February 1848, boldly proclaimed British sovereignty over the territory between the Orange and the Vaal. Pretorius mustered a commando and led it to Bloemfontein; Smith gathered his men and attacked successfully in a 'smart little action' at Boomplatz on 29 August, 'one of the severest skirmishes I ever saw', after which Pretorius withdraw across the Vaal.

Three years of Smith's vigorous administration followed, marred only by a few flurries such as that caused by his suggesting importing convict labour, and the repeated Kaffir struggles on both frontiers. By the time of Smith's recall in 1852, the Sand River Convention was moving to establish the independence of the Transvaal, a complicated business, as the area consisted of four separate districts (Zoutpansberg, Utrecht, Lydenburg and Potchefstroom), but eventually

they fused into one, the four districts being commemor-
ated in the Vierkleur flag, which was, and is, the Netherlands tricolour with a wide green stripe along the hoist. In
1864 Pretorius became the President, ten years after another
Convention at Bloemfontein created the Orange Free State.

The 1860s were marred, or enlivened, according to the
onlooker's viewpoint, by a most spectacular wrangle in
church affairs. As described by Mr Morris it was started,
unspectacularly enough, by Robert Gray, first Bishop of
Cape Town, who, arriving in 1847, found that his diocese
covered an area of over 250,000 square miles served by a
total of thirteen Anglican clergy who had 'failed to dent the
mountain of work that had to be done'. By 1852 Gray
petitioned for the creation of two new bishoprics, Natal and
Grahamstown, and selected, for Natal, John Colenso, the
thirty-eight year old vicar of Forncett Saint Mary in Norfolk, author of a mathematics textbook that had now become
standard in schools and of a book of sermons that showed
his allegiance to the theories of one Frederick Denison
Maurice, 'widely regarded as little more than a muddle-
minded mystic'. Consecrated at Lambeth in the presence of
six bishops on 30 November 1853, Colenso sailed two weeks
later, made a whirlwind ten-week tour of Natal during
which he met hundreds of people and made an excellent
impression, came home in May 1854 to raise money for
church and mission expansion, and was settled at Bishop-
stowe near Pietermaritzburg by September 1855. Over the
next seven years he broke completely with Gray, whose ambition was to establish an independent and High Anglican
diocese, whereas Colenso was Low in belief and practice,
and, what was more, felt with the majority of Anglicans in
Southern Africa a profound aversion to 'a High Church
body with no civil barrier between it and Rome'. Worst of
all, at a moment when the Darwinian controversy was at
its height, Colenso published, with singularly ill-advised
timing, the first of his seven-volume analysis of the Scrip-
tures, which, dealing principally with factual errors, shocked
the establishment into thinking that he was set upon
destroying the Bible. Colenso was tried for heresy in Cape
Town, Gray making the arrangements hurriedly and rush-
ing through an adverse verdict, which naturally caused
public opinion to veer back towards its victim.

The whole affair dragged on for years, petering out only

when Gray died in 1872, by which time Colenso had become a tourist attraction in Pietermaritzburg. Before that there had been many lively developments, including Colenso's lawsuit for his stipend against the trustees, one of whom was Mr Gladstone, and Gray's reading out from the altar steps of Colenso's own cathedral the sentence of Greater Excommunication against him, which had only the effect of splitting Pietermaritzburg into opposing camps. The creation of a new Bishopric of Maritzburg, and the installation of William Macrorie, followed almost at once by an accusation of pederasty against one of Gray's supporters, Bishop Twells (who fled over the border in disguise), kept the pot boiling, but by the time Gray died the original issues had long since been submerged in a downpour of judgments, pronouncements, verdicts, ideas, opinions and legal documentation.

On a lighter note, Ogilvie's football, known as Gog's Game from the only legible bit of the Canon's signature, reached its first point of fulfilment in March 1875 with the formation of the first rugby club in the southern hemisphere, the Hamilton RFC. Gog's Game persisted for a while, but by 1878 it had become true Rugby Union, and in that year W. M. Milton, an English International, who later as Sir William Milton became Governor of Rhodesia, arrived at the Cape. Rugby went from strength to strength, with a great boom in Kimberley between 1883 and 1886, until in 1891 Mr (later Sir) Donald Currie of the Castle Shipping Line offered a gold cup to be presented to the best opposition to the first British team to visit South Africa. With financial backing from a wealthy immigrant named Rhodes, the team sailed on the *Dunottar Castle* on Saturday 20 June, docking at Cape Town after a record-breaking voyage of sixteen days. The team travelled to various parts of the country in coasters, trains as far as the lines would go, and a coach drawn by ten ponies, slept on hut floors, played their matches on hard grassless ground covered in red dust, and started a pattern that apart from several vicissitudes has persisted to this day. The first tennis club in Natal was started by Mrs James Hackland in 1884, with eight courts. Her husband had repaired wagons for Rhodes in Natal before Rhodes went on to Kimberley. Mrs Hackland, not content with tennis, also started the first South African croquet club.

The British to Southern Africa

After the makers of progress spiritual and temporal, the destroyers. All this time the Army had not been idle. The so-called Kaffir Wars were finally fought to a climax, but no sooner had that smouldering fire been stamped out in 1877 than the Zulu under their great chief Cetewayo burst out in Natal. They defeated the British at Isandhlwana, fought them to something of a stalemate at Rorke's Drift, and, in a minor action, killed the Prince Imperial of France: possibly altering European history considerably. Isandhlwana itself was less of a shock to England, where the Prince Imperial's death was the news story of the year; but the English reaction paled before the fury that roared out of France, where the whole thing was seen as a dastardly plot, Perfidious Albion at its worst. English travellers and businessmen scuttled home for shelter, or hid themselves inside their shuttered offices.

Clearly Cetewayo and his impis had to be stopped. The British Colonial Secretary, the fourth Earl of Carnarvon, who had created the federation of the North American provinces, was equally interested in federation of the South African ones, and found the Zulu the main obstacle in that path. He was able and hard-working, but stubborn; at the age of seven he had made his first speech (to the RSPCA, of which his father was president); and his colleagues called him 'Twitters'. None the less, he was going to start the process that eventually changed South Africa into a country instead of a motley collection of two British provinces, two Boer republics, and an indefinite scattering of native kingdoms. His first moves brought trouble. He sent James Anthony Froude, the celebrated historian, to Cape Town to preach federation, but Froude fell foul of both the Governor, Sir Henry Barkly, and the Prime Minister, Sir John Molteno, the former railway-maker. Carnarvon therefore turned his attention to Natal, whose elderly Governor, Sir Benjamin Chilley Pine, was gently coasting towards retirement, and replaced him by the most spectacular military figure of the moment, Major-General Sir Garnet Joseph Wolseley, GCMG, KCB, who had served in the Crimea and the Indian Mutiny, became a general before he was forty, was intolerant, practical, self-confident and eager for Army reform, and whose opponents were many and eminent. He reached Natal in April 1879, and within three months the Zulu had been brought to their last decisive battle.

The British forces on this occasion were commanded by Lord Chelmsford, also a Crimea veteran, who hated South Africa and most of the people he met there. His troops were a peculiar mixture, starting with the usual core of regulars: men who slept lying like eighteen spokes of a wheel in each big bell-tent, carried fifty-seven pounds of accoutrements on the march including seventy rounds of ammunition, a Martini-Henry rifle, and a triangular bayonet known as a lunger, and were supplied by enormous, cumbersome wagon trains each holding 1,500 tons of stocks. He also had units of local mounted troops calling themselves Rangers, Carbineers, Irregulars or Mounted Rifles, whose equipment and competence were as uneven as their names, some fine Mounted Police, 216 excellent Frontier Light Horse commanded by a man named Redvers Buller, and various individuals including two of Shepstone's sons, William Drummond riding the Prince Imperial's horse Percy, Evelyn Wood, Horace Smith-Dorrien, and Drury Lowe, commanding the Seventeenth Lancers, whose predecessors had gone to glory at Balaclava.

Chelmsford, whose natural wish in that wild difficult terrain was for a quick decisive action, confronted the mass of the Zulu at Ulundi, site of Cetewayo's kraal near the White Umfolozi River, where he did the next best thing to forming a Boer *laager*: he drew up a British square, as Wellington had done at Waterloo. The Zulu attack was noisy rather than deadly dangerous, and Buller sat motionless on his horse and smoked cigarettes while a young man called Melton Prior spent the whole of the battle busily sketching. When the square was ringed with Zulu dead and the élan of their charges was visibly weakening, Chelmsford waved his helmet and ordered :'Go at them, Lowe! ' and the Lancers, followed by the mounted volunteers, moved out, shook into line, lowered their pennon-trimmed lances to the rest and charged in a textbook action that broke Cetewayo's power for ever. Ten British were killed and sixty-nine wounded; the Zulu dead were never counted, but more than a thousand lay where the troops had ridden, and the outline of the square was precisely marked by a thick line of 35,000 spent cartridges. Chelmsford took his men down to the banks of the Mbilane River to rest and eat; many officers produced bottles of champagne, somewhat warm by now. Then they went back to mop up Ulundi. As the horses raced forward, Buller shouted: 'Who's to be first in?' and one trooper thenceforward known as 'Ulundi' Beresford for the rest of his life put his horse at the thorn hedge of the ninety-acre kraal and sailed over. The kraal was set ablaze, some few remaining Zulu dispatched or chased off (not before they had killed William Drummond), and the day's work was done. Wolseley, who had brought the medals out with him, awarded eleven Victoria Crosses for Rorke's Drift, absolutely the record for a single battle. This was increased by two in 1907, the first posthumous awards of the V.C. There was also a rash of promotions, and the Seventeenth Lancers had justified their existence for the next generation.

But already something of far more significance for Southern Africa had happened. On the banks of the Orange River some Boer children named Jacobz were playing with pebbles. One of these stones, sparkling in the sun, caught the attention of two passers-by, John O'Reilly, a hunter, and Schalk van Niekerk, a farmer. Dissatisfied with a Colesberg chemist's report that the stone was worthless, they sent it to a British immigrant, Dr Guybon Atherstone of Grahamstown, who said it was a fine diamond. Two years later, an African witch-doctor found another, much bigger, for which, to his surprise, van Niekerk gave him 500 sheep. This stone turned out to be the Star of Africa, which, sold for £11,000 and later fetching £25,000, was laid on the table of the Cape House of Assembly by the Cape Colonial Secretary, Sir Richard Southey, with the prescient words: 'Gentlemen, this is the rock on which the future success of South Africa will be built.' The year was 1869.

3. Diamonds and Gold

Sooner or later all immigrant lands develop a story-book locality. In the case of Southern Africa, this was Kimberley.

Named after the British Colonial Secretary, the place started as a tent encampment around the 'big hole' where the diggers scrabbled ever deeper. Wooden shacks, hastily assembled from packing cases and often so fragile that they could be turned round during the night, or even picked up and put down somewhere else to the angry bewilderment of the hungover owner in the morning, gave protection, more or less, against torrential rains, clouds of red dust, bitter winter nights of cold so intense that water froze in the buckets, and noon summer sun so hot that husky mineworkers fainted. Kimberley was haunted by the spectre of drought: fresh water cost a shilling a bucket and those who struck it rich preferred to take their baths in soda-water costing five shillings a bottle. According to Mr Brian Gardner and Mr Stanley Jackson, fresh vegetables were sometimes priced at ten shillings each, cabbages thirty shillings, potatoes four shillings a pound, 'a half-crown onion was a luxury'; sugar at half a crown a pound 'remained scarce'. Every item of stores had to come by the thirty-five day cart-journey from the Cape or (at equally exorbitant prices) from Boer farmers who not unnaturally seized the opportunity, while at the same time execrating the horde of 'godless and greedy invaders' who turned the area into Sodom and Gomorrah, dreamed of overnight fortunes and (worse) made them, and corrupted the African workers with guns and the raw brandy known as Cape Smoke.

These godless invaders numbered over ten thousand by late 1871 and included, Mr Jackson found, prospectors from rushes in America and Australia, professional gamblers, actors and boxers, as well as 'Fenians, German speculators, rabbis, ex-convicts, cashiered soldiers and the inevitable camp followers . . . Grahamstown cathedral lost its organist and most of the choir' and the son of the Bishop himself. They drank uproariously in the Occidental Bar and the Fountain Bar, had their photographs taken in Caney's Portrait Rooms, played roulette in Dodd's Bar where whisky and cigars were issued free to players, and made spirited bids for Cape Town girls in the saloons. Every man, including the doctors on their rounds, carried firearms; one of these doctors, a lively Scot, driving his two black horses to a smart victoria, was highly popular in Kimberley: Dr Leander Starr Jameson.

A small, stocky young man with black hair and spaniel eyes, with a magnetic personality and a ready laugh. 'Dr Jim' had hero-worshipped empire-builders like Robert Clive since his schooldays and longed for the chance of some daring exploit that would make him famous. When mine-owners panicked over a worker's smallpox symptoms and feared a strike among the other Africans, Jameson blithely diagnosed 'a bulbous disease of the skin'. Fellow doctors disagreed and a scandal buzzed round Kimberley that took Jameson some time to live down. He still had the town's best practice, however, and was considered a very good surgeon and physician. He had come to Africa for his health, and was picked by another immigrant as a doctor he could trust. This was perhaps the most celebrated Briton ever to settle in the continent: Cecil John Rhodes.

Born at Bishop's Stortford on 5 July 1853, one of the twelve children of a vicar, Rhodes was educated at the local grammar school because he was too delicate for Eton or Winchester like his brothers. He dreamed of going to Oxford and becoming a clergyman or a barrister, but his tuberculosis forced him to seek a warm climate. His brother Herbert was growing cotton in Natal and Rhodes joined him in 1870, aged seventeen, an awkward reserved young man with ruffled tawny hair and bony wrists that stuck too far out of his shrunken school blazer. His capital was two thousand pounds borrowed from an aunt. His first impression of Africa was 'very rum'. Africa eventually concluded the same of him.

Rumours of diamonds led him to make the 400-mile journey to Kimberley in an ox-cart, where he joined the gangs of diggers and naked natives hacking and scraping at 'the big Stilton cheese'. The diggers laughed at his beaky nose and squeaky voice and thought him peculiar because he stayed alone. He sat on an upturned bucket sorting his finds and reading Virgil. He dug hard and sieved patiently, and almost at once he began to find diamonds. He had lucky escapes from fall-ins but broke his right little finger carrying a bucket; it never set properly and left him with a limp handshake that went well with his brusque, shy manner. Mr Jackson describes how at the end of the day he would trot away over the moonlit veld on 'a rusty pony' with 'an odd tailless dog' padding beside him. For years his quarters were in a shack where he slept on an iron bedstead with a Gladstone bag bolstering the pillow. In addition to Virgil he had a Greek lexicon and a copy of Marcus Aurelius. As soon as he saw his way clear he sailed for England to keep his first term at Oxford, travelling first-class though his one pair of faded flannels had to be patched with canvas by the ship's sailmaker. On the way the passengers crowded to the rails to watch the *Anglian* go by on her maiden voyage to the Cape, which she made in the record-breaking total of twenty-seven days.

On board the *Anglian* was a young man with thirty pounds, forty boxes of cigars, a second-hand nickel watch bought by his old school friends for twenty-five shillings, a flashy suit, a bowler and a cane—a blue-eyed, pink-faced, golden-haired Cockney of twenty-one (exactly a year older than Rhodes), named Barnett Isaacs. He and his brother Harry, brought up in poverty in the East End, had become expert street traders and competent boxers, and Barney was also a skilful conjurer. A quiet, sober cousin called David Harris, who had studied commerce and literature, paid the brothers a visit in 1871 and announced that he was going to South Africa—'Here are diamonds. Millions!' Harry followed David later, starting off as an entertainer, but did badly; at last he got a job behind the counter of merchant Van Praagh and wrote asking Barney to join him. An old childhood joke, '——and Barney too', gave this new immigrant his name of Barney Barnato.

Barnato could not pay the forty-pound fare for the coach journey to Kimberley, but within a week of arriving in Cape Town he had found a wagon-driver who would take him to the diamonds for five pounds. They took two months. There were floods and chilly nights and blistered feet, but Barnato, singing music-hall songs and waving his bowler to passing Boers, felt light-hearted. He remained so throughout the difficult days, with Harry ill, trading uncertain and the future inscrutable. He sold the cigars slowly, box by box; he sold his watch-works for five shillings but kept the case to hold diamonds later. In the 'dusty fly-blown mass of pits between mounds of gravel' he sparkled and entertained; Mr Jackson truly commented that 'only a man of stout heart with an elephantine hide could have survived' among the treeless camps of mud and dust with not a blade of grass visible for miles, where the diamond-fever was such that sailors deserted their ships to join—one known as Champagne Charlie salted his first claim with a broken glass bottle-stopper. No one at first was allowed more than a single claim of thirty-one square feet, sombrely referred to as 'ten times the size of your grave', but soon syndicates began among the 'kopje-wallopers'. Barnato teamed up with Louis Cohen of Liverpool, living in a corrugated-iron shed nine feet by six, furnished with a trestle table and scales, pliers, a magnifying glass, a watchmaker's glass (Barnato was one of the first to use one in Kimberley), and two borrowed stools that had to be returned to the bar every night; they slept on a straw mattress with one green blanket that Cohen regularly pulled away, and might run on a Saturday night to a sixpenny bowl of 'thick flyblown soup'.

The pair become known for having fairly balanced scales. For months they worked harder than anyone, picking up small stones; came the blissful week when their profit was ninety pounds. Barnato kept healthy by shadow-boxing and exercising with Indian clubs outside the shack each morning, finishing off with a sluice-down from a bucket of cold water. He built up a fast, highly efficient intelligence service; like Rhodes he believed the diamonds lay thickest in the blue ground, not the yellow. He was right: early in 1876 he bought four adjoining claims from the two Kerr brothers for three thousand pounds, and, sifting diamonds from an area the size of a house, soon made two thousand a week. By the end of the first year he had made ninety thousand; in under twenty years he would be worth five pounds a minute.

Kimberley was changing. The 'big hole' was over four hundred feet deep and covered with the cobweb of steel cables that had replaced the old hand-winding gear. Steam pumps made obsolete the early cradles and buckets. The first pump came up from Port Elizabeth for Rhodes: he used it to make ice cream, then charged a thousand pounds for pumping out a flooded claim with it. New brick buildings rose among the shacks, in one of which Rhodes still lived obscurely; one wall was now covered by a map of Africa sprinkled with tiny Union Jacks, for he was already dreaming of the Cape to Cairo railway and believing: 'I would annex the planets if I could—I often think of that'. From the shack he emerged to visit the British Mess, known locally as 'The Twelve Apostles'—a tin hut where the select few gossiped, drank, played cards, and smoked Boer tobacco. Rhodes, averaging a hundred pounds a week, had taken a partner, nine years older than he, Charles Rudd, son of a Norfolk landowner and shipping magnate, champion hurdler at Harrow, Cambridge Blue, who also had been sent to Africa for his health. Rhodes had chosen wisely: Rudd was dependable, loyal and brilliantly talented with finance. For eight years Rhodes commuted between Oxford and Kimberley, becoming wealthier all the time, eventually never sailing without his own cow and hens so that he could have fresh milk and eggs on the voyage; it was piquant indeed to live at such extremes, the stately intellectual dignity of the Schools and the crude scrambling shanty-town of the diamonds. With the premonition of early death that never left him (his last words were: 'So little done, so much to do'), he kept obsessionally making his will. The first of these, drawn up when he was twenty-four, is remarkable: he left his whole estate in trust to the Colonial Secretary to found 'a secret society' to 'extend British rule throughout the world', not forgetting the 'ultimate recovery' of the United States to the Empire. Believing the British to be the natural rulers of mankind, he never abandoned his ideal: the habitable globe colonized and governed by Britain. It may have been megalomaniac, but it was not ignoble.

Exclaiming jubilantly: 'Four million engagement rings a year, and each one worth at least a pound a carat!' Rhodes realized that he must control the main mine. This was on a farm nicely named Foresight ('Vooruitzigt') bought for fifty pounds in 1860 by a Boer called De Beers. Rhodes and Rudd, aided by Alfred Beit, another financial genius who became their most trusted adviser, began buying up claims, securing De Beers for £6,500 (they later sold it to the government for £ 00,000). Rhodes believed that every man had his price, a theory from which results did nothing to deter him, and gained eventual control of the Kimberley complex through his qualities of toughness, obstinacy, the ability to select and manage useful men, and unscrupulous business sense.

Gradually it became clear that the biggest obstacle in the path of Rhodes was Barnato, who had amassed a tremendous fortune before he had been in the country ten years. Unlike Rhodes, Barnato was gregarious: he formed and patronized the Turf Club and the drama society, where he met a young immigrant actress, Fanny Bees, who married him (unofficially) in 1877 (officially in London in November 1892), and brought out two nephews to enjoy the benefits of diamond-mining. The first nephew was Woolf Joel, aged fifteen, possessing acute financial perception even then, who was paid fifty pounds a week plus commission and within two years had several thousand in his own bank account, so he could take a trip home first-class. The second was Woolf's elder brother Solly, who developed a passion for diamonds in themselves (he invented the De Beers advertising slogan 'a diamond is forever'); later known as King Sol, tall, elegant, smoking gold-tipped cigarettes in a long diamond-encrusted holder and keeping a solid gold replica of the Primrose Mine tower as a table decoration, he filled a wooden box two feet long with diamonds, replacing only those that were sold so that supply and demand kept rigid pace. Brother Harry in the meantime owned the London Hotel opposite Jameson's surgery, which was convenient for treating the drunks Harry bounced out. Cousin David was a successful though modest broker, married (surprisingly) to his shipboard romance and possibly the happiest of all.

Rhodes brought a Rothschild into partnership, agreed with Beit that Barnato was 'an impossible person', and saw his dream of imperial glory wrecked by 'a tiresome Cockney adventurer'; Barnato thought Rhodes despised him for arriving with just a few boxes of cigars while 'he had his Greek dictionary'; but the two had still not met. When they did it was almost catastrophic: Rhodes crossly quoted Latin, provoking Barnato: 'When he talked *Greek* at me, I knew he was dotty. He thinks he's Kimberley's bloody messiah.' Rhodes calmed down and tried the subtle approach, telling

Diamonds and Gold

Beit and Jameson: 'He wants to be an MP as well as a member of the Kimberley Club. God knows why! But if he wants it, let him have it', and, most spectacular of all, inviting Barnato with Harris and Solly to see the De Beers collection. Laid out in 160 piles exquisitely graded by size, shape and quality on tissue paper in a long shallow trough, they had taken six weeks to sort and totalled over 200,000 carats. Barnato agreed to come in at Rhodes' price of £700,000, whereupon Rhodes, determined to give De Beers a breathing-space, tipped up the trough so the jewels cascaded into a bucket, and said: 'Now let's walk down to your office with it and make the people stare'. This they did, swinging the bucket between them, along Kimberley's main street, watched by (among many) the new kind of broker, lounging at his office door resplendent in velvet coat, white buckskin breeches, and polished spurred boots. Uncounted numbers of diamonds went on being stolen, smuggled out in increasingly ingenious ways: fastened to carrier pigeons flown across the border, fed in meat to starving dogs; but there were plenty more where those came from.

De Beers Consolidated Mines Limited was established on 13 March 1888 with a cheque for £5,338,650 that hangs today in a frame on the boardroom wall. Barnato's reward was election to the Cape Assembly after a campaign he conducted wearing a pale grey coat and driving a coach and four with six liveried horsemen in green and gold: Kimberley's first, and so far most spectacular, election. Rhodes was already Member for Barkly West, elected in 1881 and taking his seat wearing English tweeds for once in preference to his usual white flannels, shabby coat and tennis shoes that often led strangers to misjudge him. One Afrikaner politician did not make that mistake: 'This young man will cause trouble if he does not leave politics alone and turn to something else'.

This shrewd verdict was given in 1885 at Fourteen Springs, first meeting of Rhodes and the speaker, who was President of the Transvaal, a heavy solid legend in black, puffing morosely at a long pipe, resting his elbow on a thick Dutch Bible, from time to time sucking his maimed thumb, the top of which he had cut off with his own knife when his rifle exploded out hunting; he had gone on the Great Trek as a boy of eleven, believed that the earth was flat and that hymn-singing was sinfully frivolous, hated foreigners, had sixteen children, always spoke Afrikaans except in prayer when he used High Dutch to favour the Almighty with his confidences, and was called uncle by his people, though his full name was Stephanus Johannes Paulus Kruger.

Kruger disliked Rhodes before he ever met him, and saw no reason to change his mind after, but he rather surprisingly got on well with the brash and ebullient Barnato, who spent hours chatting with him on the stoep of Kruger's Pretoria house, its entrance still dominated by the two stone lions given him by Barnato on his seventy-first birthday. Kruger detested the goings-on in Kimberley but hated even more the similar events in what he called the devil's city when the gold of the Rand was discovered in 1868, making the Transvaal the most sought-after piece of land on earth.

The first payable gold came up at the piously named Natalia mine in Eersteling, whose tall chimney-stack became mythical: the Boers came to believe that when it fell so would British power in South Africa, and once they yoked a double span of oxen to the chimney and pulled; but Dr Oliver Ransford saw it still standing in 1967. But the thick seams of gold ran under the ridge of white waters, the Witwatersrand. Here sprang up the city of gold, Johannesburg, today described by Mr James Cameron as 'brash, vulgar, neurotic, rich, crime-ridden', surrounded by the beautiful silver-grey, golden-fawn dumps, with over a hundred parks and dozens of tennis courts, though a century ago there was not a tree in sight. Here came the prospectors in their open shirts, moleskin trousers, slouch hats and riding-boots, carrying pistols as a matter of course and speaking their jargon of bonanzas, panning-out, lucky strikes, bedrock, staking claims and going stony-broke.

It was like Kimberley all over again—wagons, tents, huts and camp-fires on the cracked red earth, tin shacks almost melting in the heat or swimming in summer cloudbursts, no sanitation, no street lighting, the Grand Hotel with bedrooms hurriedly built up in tin and matchwood tiers, potatoes costing five shillings a bucket, firewood twenty-eight shillings a load, small tins of butter three shillings each; the first bank was a mud-thatched hut with no strongroom and only a few six-shooters to guard the deposits. Crowds of hopeful fortune-hunters flocked to the Rand with the usual scallywags and hangers-on, and these Outlanders set up the problem that would bring the immigrants to war. No wonder

The Zulu War: General Newdigate addressing the Lancers before the Battle of Ulundi, 1879 (from a sketch by Melton Prior)

Kruger hated it. On one of the few occasions when he could be persuaded to visit Johannesburg he began his speech: 'Burghers, friends, murderers, thieves and robbers'. As he saw it, his people had won the country with blood and endurance; they had travelled far and struggled through every sort of obstacle to find sanctuary for their way of life, and now here they were confronting a horde of mixed and mercenary worldlings whose whole make-up was diametrically opposed to their own and who might in a short time outnumber them. He sincerely believed that if he gave them any privileges he 'might as well haul down the Vierkleur'.

Both Rhodes and Barnato came late on the scene (though when they did their Midas touch still worked: both made new fortunes), as they had been preoccupied with the merger, their elections, and their steadily increasing wealth. Barnato, for example, was making £50,000 a year by 1885; as early as 1880 his company shares on the four original claims, valued at £100,000, were subscribed twice over inside an hour and his own holdings trebled within a few weeks. But Rhodes had also been busy with something else: the opening-up of the territory that was to bear his name.

Rhodesian history, like that of the Union, moves upwards from the Cape; and when Henry Hartley and Karl Mauch found a vein of gold in Mashonaland, tremors of excitement began to run among treasure-dreamers. The first step was to secure concessions, just as Fynn and Farewell had done fifty years before, from the local monarch, in this case Mzilikaze's heir. Mzilikaze had actually died in his bed, in 1868, aged nearly eighty; the present king was a fat man with a blue monkey-skin kilt and sixty-eight wives, known in government despatches as Lo Bengula and to the settlers as Old Lob. The artist-explorer Thomas Baines secured a concession for the Tati area in 1869, which brought other concession hunters, known as 'The White Sharks' or 'Lob's Foreign Legion', swooping down like vultures. Confused, Old Lob valiantly held them off, balancing uneasily among them, until Rhodes sent up John Smith Moffat, son of Robert, to negotiate; Lobengula set his mark to a treaty on 11 February 1888. Since the risk of his backsliding still bothered Rhodes, eight months later Rudd went up with James Maguire and Frank Thompson, to clinch the vital mining-rights. Rudd gave Lobengula a hundred gold sove-

reigns and arranged an imposing visit from the Bechuanaland Deputy Administrator, Sir Sydney Shippard, whose
formal frock-coat and escort of Border Police impressed all
who saw them. Rudd got his rights with full powers 'to do
all the things that might be deemed necessary to win and
procure the same' at the small cost of £100 a month paid
to Lobengula, 1,000 rifles with 100,000 rounds of ammunition, and the promise of a gunboat on the Zambesi. In 1889
Queen Victoria granted the Charter of the British South
Africa Company which, Rhodes said, was intended to 'promote trade, civilization and good government, and check
the slave trade'. Aghast at what he thought was a piece of
sharp practice against the heir of the king who had so
rightly trusted his own father, Moffat wrote to Rhodes
uncompromisingly:

> I feel bound to tell you that I look on the whole plan
> as detestable, whether viewed in the light of policy or
> morality. When Lobengula finds it all out, as he is sure
> to do sooner or later, what faith will he have in you?

Lobengula did find out, and was furious. Shippard wrote:

> Lo Bengula's present position is most difficult and
> dangerous . . . He is sharp enough and farsighted
> enough to understand that the English alliance might
> be his best card if only he could trust the English, but
> there's the rub. England has a bad name in South
> Africa for breaking faith with natives.

He also reported that Lobengula had said: 'England is the
chameleon and I am that fly'.

Rhodes, who had no wish to see the gold of Mashonaland
go unsupervised into the pockets of any casual treasure-
hunters, knew that some were asking Lobengula's permission direct to go prospecting. When, as Mr Frank Clements
found out, 'some Australians who arrived in Durban to
learn that the latest El Dorado lay a thousand miles away
became so dangerously enraged that troops had to be
brought in to protect the town', Rhodes played his trump
card. He sent Jameson to Bulawayo with instructions to use
all his charm 'and anything else he could think of' to keep
Lobengula sweet. Jameson succeeded, partly by bringing a

deputation carrying a letter from the Queen and escorted by troopers in full dress, partly by telling Lobengula that all great men had gout—he treated the king for this, also for dropsy. When the Charter was signed, protests burst out in England against such power being given to a profit-making concern. One of the loudest voices was that of Henry Labouchere, Editor of *Truth*, who called Rhodes 'an empire jerry-builder who was the head of a gang of shady financiers'.

Rhodes paid not the slightest attention. He was busy organizing his Pioneer Column to occupy the new, enormous territory. Their route was suggested and plotted by a hunter who knew the interior well, Frederick Courteney Selous, who also proposed that the Pioneers should number about two hundred. Sir Henry Loch, British High Commissioner at the Cape, insisted that five hundred mounted police should go along as well to protect the column and set up strong-points on the way, though he wrote to Rhodes: 'The object to be obtained is the peaceful occupation of Mashonaland.' The 187 successful applicants, less than a tenth of those who asked to go, trained at Mafeking with weapons, uniforms and horses supplied by Rhodes, who paid them their keep plus more than seven times the daily pay of the British regular. They included lawyers and clergymen, farmers, engineers, builders, butchers and printers. Frank Lawson was contractor-organizer; Colonel Pennefather was column commander; A. R. Colquhoun was Mashonaland administrator; the top man was Jameson himself. One of the police escort, Major Leonard, described them as:

> such a mixed lot I never saw in my life, all sorts and conditions from the aristocrat to the street arab, peers and the waifs of humanity mingling together like the ingredients in a hotch-potch.

They included a survivor of the Charge of the Light Brigade, young men out for adventure, some American scouts from the Indian wars, one American named William Harvey Brown whose farm, on the site of the present-day Salisbury airport, was called Arlington, misfits and pillars of society, all filled with self-confident and lively spirit. Brushing aside native raiders and Boer protesters alike, they made their march in eleven weeks and on 12 September 1890 they halted at Harari, renamed it Fort Salisbury in honour of the British Prime Minister, hoisted the Union Jack and launched Rhodesia without the loss of a single life. Cecil Square in Salisbury is on the site of the first Pioneer camp, and Pioneers Day is a public holiday every 12 September.

It was not all smooth, however: raids sputtered up between the Pioneers on the one hand and the Mashona and Matabele on the other for the next three years until Jameson and Rhodes brought the killings to a halt. The first base camp was Fort Victoria and an Order in Council of May 1891 placed the Company's territory under the Queen's protection, but the Mashona and Matabele had not read it. Jameson at first telegraphed lightheartedly to Rhodes: 'The Victoria people have naturally got the jumps but I hope to get rid of the Matabele without trouble'; and wrote to his brother: 'The surroundings of the Chartered's . . . I shall do my best to increase, in fact all of the so-called Zambezia or as it will be called "Rhodesia".' But when he travelled to Fort Victoria and saw villages in flames, and when Captain Allan Wilson's patrol of thirty-three mounted troopers died to the last man on the Shangani (the most famous single incident in Rhodesian history, their Bannockburn or Bastille), he knew it was serious. According to Colonel Stevenson-Hamilton, 'Ignorant people at home cried out at our "brutality" in conquering those fiends of hell', and Labouchere referred to the Pioneers as 'border ruffians', as some of them were: some freebooters went in for 'highway robbery, rustling, illicit diamond dealing and whatever else offered profit', and there was 'Scotty' Smith who had a private army of thirty British and sixty Zulu; Major Leonard wrote: 'There is a strong vein of the bully in us fairplay-loving islanders in spite of all the cant we talk', and according to one Blakiston: 'Everyone in Mashonaland is either slave to Mammon or Bacchus'. Blakiston died at Lonely Mine in the rising, and has a school and a street in Salisbury named after him.

Eventually Rhodes himself came up to settle the question. He rode everywhere (though he was considered atrocious on horseback), and his real achievement was the two months of meetings, when he faced the tribal leaders unarmed and persuaded them to accept peace: there is nothing to compare with this in African history. Lobengula had taken refuge in the bush where eventually he died obscurely on 22

January 1894, after Major Patrick William Forbes had led a double column against Bulawayo; the town was occupied, with bagpipes playing among the smoking ruins, on 4 November 1893. In the wreckage of Old Lob's capital Rhodes addressed the Pioneers:

> You will be the first entitled to select land, and you will deal with it after provision has been made for the natives. It is your right, for you have conquered the country.

In this new untouched place, with its clear hot sunshine, cool nights, spectacular sunsets, the fabled land of Ophir and King Solomon's Mines (though actual mining there was always chancy, as shown by mine names: 'Cross your Luck', 'Clean Up', 'Broke'), Rhodes ordered that the towns of Salisbury and Bulawayo should have streets broad enough to allow an eight-pair team of oxen to turn comfortably. Lobengula, however, is not forgotten: Bulawayo's coat of arms today bears the royal Matabele emblem of three rock-rabbits and Lobengula's own device, the elephant, and its motto, 'Let us go forward', is in his language; he remains the only African to have a European street named after him; but Salisbury (which contains the only statue of Rhodes sculpted from life) has a Latin motto meaning, somewhat ominously, 'In discrimination there is safety'.

Of the opening-up Mr Clements has said: 'Deceit and bribery prepared the way for successful violence', though, of course, 'the same could be said of Caesar's Gaul'.

Meanwhile, back on the Rand, the trouble had come. Kruger and his Volksraad steadfastly refused to grant the franchise to the Outlanders, although they paid nine-tenths of the taxes and were the cause of the Transvaal's prosperity. Among the taxes they paid was, ironically enough, a poll-tax, also a miners' tax estimated to have raised costs by two dollars for every ton of rock shifted. Kruger pushed through a stream of laws restricting the vote to those who had lived in the country for fourteen years, been naturalized for twelve during which they had of course forfeited their vote at home, and were aged at least forty, virtually putting the franchise out of the question. Despite the Queen's proclamation of Transvaal sovereignty, this was violated in 1877 when Sir Theophilus Shepstone, the same who had gone up to Griqua Town aged three and who was now Secretary for Native Affairs and a weightily dignified elder of awesome presence, rode into Pretoria with twenty-five policemen and a few civil servants, one of whom was Rider Haggard, and simply took over the country. At first the Boers seemed too stunned to act, while their creditors and the Outlanders were naturally delighted, but then Boer support began to crystallize round the indomitable Kruger, who fought for his beleaguered republic with all his cunning, holding out for union on his own terms and threatening to call Germany to his aid against the wicked British. Towards the Outlanders he remained implacable: they had not been invited, if they disliked it they could go—he was not stopping them. Petitions broke harmlessly at the foot of his rocklike will; to one deputation he said simply: 'Go back and tell your people I shall never give them anything: I shall never change my policy, and now let the storm burst'. Burst it did.

Shepstone was replaced by Colonel Sir Owen Lanyon, described by Dr Ransford as a 'cranky paper-shuffling fusspot' who wanted to run the country as if it were a regiment. He paid little attention to mumblings in the Transvaal about a war of liberation during most of 1880. In October of that year the first train from Durban steamed into Pretoria, the Natal Government having pushed its incredible line, with gradients as steep as one in thirty, that far; on the footplate was Lady Colley, the Governor's wife. Major-General Sir George Pomerory-Colley, KCSI, CB, CMG, aged forty-five, educated at Sandhurst and chosen to write the article on the British Army for the ninth edition of the Encyclopaedia Britannica, who took sketchbooks everywhere he went, wrote bad verse, played the small accordion and read Ruskin, had been appointed in July. Sent by Wolseley to confer with President Burgers of the Transvaal, his route passed his future grave and he now had four months to live, for the South African War had a prelude, or dress rehearsal, nearly twenty years in advance, from which nobody apparently learnt anything.

It began at Potchefstroom—'the emotional heart and driving centre of Calvinism in South Africa', Mr John Cope calls it—where willow-trees had been imported from China to shade the river-banks. A burgher called, almost, it seemed, inevitably, Bezuidenhout was sent a summons for £27 5s. back tax. He proved that he only owed £14, and agreed to pay that provided it could be credited to the future republican government; the local magistrate ordered him to pay the costs as well, which neatly totalled £13 5s. Bezuidenhout refused, the court distrained on his wagon, and a local mob led by a critical citizen named Piet Cronje hijacked the wagon and called a meeting at Paardekraal where they proclaimed the republic, chose a triumvirate provisional government of Kruger, Joubert and Pretorius, and finished off the day's work by piling up a stone cairn with a Vierkleur on top and deciding to announce the new government officially on the anniversary of Blood River, a week away. The nearest printer was at Potchefstroom; 500 Boers rode in on 15 December and found 140 British infantrymen uneasily trying to feel for some sort of order. The Boers jeered, scuffles broke out, shots cracked, and the British retreated to their fort. Those shots started the First Boer War, and arguments still rage over who fired first.

There was no doubt who fired next. Franz Joubert took a commando of 200 Boers to ambush Colonel Anstruther's column, ordered up to reinforce Pretoria. Some thirty-six miles short of its destination the Boers found the column, 250 strong, strung out for over a mile, some wives and children in the baggage wagons at the back, the regimental band playing in front and the men singing and eating peaches as they swung along towards a small stream known as Bronkhorst Spruit, just before 1 p.m. on 20 December. Within a few minutes 120 soldiers lay dead or wounded, and the injured Anstruther mumbled an order to his bugler to sound the cease-fire. The Boers lost two killed, five wounded. They were chivalrous to the survivors, and buried the dead at the roadside (where legend stated that the peaches in their pockets grew into a line of fruit-trees), and Colley was ordered up on Christmas Day to teach the Boers a lesson.

It took him nearly a month to concentrate his troops at Newcastle, thirty miles short of the Transvaal border, because, he said, they had been 'scattered in penny packets in isolated garrisons all over the country', but on 24 January he was ready to move up the main road with his young, untried, appallingly bad shots. In torrential rain they trudged slowly up to the low broad saddle of Laing's Nek, backed by its semicircle of hills dominated by the flat-topped Hill of the Doves, a haunted place. Laing's Nek, in the sunshine of 28 January, was the last assault of the redcoats, the last time British regimental colours were carried into battle, and it was a failure: Colonel Deane led the attack, in which nearly all the officers were shot at once (one fell shouting 'Floreat Etona!'), and 150 British died compared with 14 Boers. Ten days later Colley's men at Ingogo were scattered in a storm by rifle fire so accurate that Colley was sure he was outnumbered three to one, again losing 150 men, while the Boers lost eight. Lord Kimberley promptly proposed armistice negotiations, but Colley, led by his doom to have one last try, kept the orders back until he was ready to move again, this time against the Hill of the Doves, known as Majuba.

This was an even bigger disaster. Rider Haggard, then ostrich-farming near Newcastle, thought Colley was 'not himself' when he planned it. The troops assembled at Mount Prospect had a lively day on 26 February, playing cricket and listening to the band and the pipers, and that night set out for the summit of Majuba, about 600 men though reports all differ: an eerie nervous march with detachments dropped on the way to guard the approach. By five on Sunday morning 365 soldiers had scrambled breathlessly up the painfully steep slopes and flung themselves flat on the grass, but Colley did not set them to dig trenches, nor did he explain that they were in that ten-acre triangle to turn the Boer flank, so they relaxed and slept while Colley sent flag and heliograph signals asking for groceries and reinforcements. Alerted by a woman, Mrs de Jager, from her farm on the western slope, the Boers planned and moved swiftly and brilliantly, opening fire soon after midday. One Boer, over 900 yards away, mortally wounded Colley's second-in-command, the only man whose advice Colley might have heeded. Attacking at the hill's weakest point, the Boers created panic so that by a quarter past one it was all over bar the killing. Colley, moving as though in a trance, was killed at last; altogether 280 British died, were wounded or captured, and for days afterwards, Dr Ransford found, the dead Highlanders 'festooned the hill like a grisly necklace'. The Boers lost two dead, four wounded, and two horses.

The troops waiting enviously and optimistically at Mount Prospect gradually realized that something was terribly wrong, until at last they observed the British rout through their field-glasses. When the news reached London it produced horror, rumours, and a frantic search for a scapegoat: finally the blame was squarely placed on the dead Colley. The Boers, buoyed up by serene joy and conviction of divine favour, rested at a spot where they later built the township of Volksrust. One man there was a certain Christiaan de Wet. No more fighting took place; then within a few weeks Rhodes came for the first time into an assembled Cape Legislature still smarting from the unusual and bitter taste of defeat.

It seems appropriate to describe this messy campaign in such detail because the lessons were clear for all to read, and the British did not read them. Eighteen years later they would charge into action yelling 'Remember Majuba' but that was the one thing the British top brass had not done. The Duke of Cambridge complained that his men had been defeated by 'an army of deerstalkers', but no one really seemed to have taken the measure of the fighting Boers. Gathered up into loose units known as commandos under elected Field-Cornets, without uniforms, without heroics, without any orthodox military structure, they were simply a collection of individuals who thought war was a citizen's unpleasant duty. There was no glory in dying on the battle-field: far more practical and sensible to live to fight another day. High in morale, they believed in their special providence, the predikants assured them they were fighting under General Jesus, they loved their country and were determined to keep it. Their way of life had made them incredibly accurate shots. Yet Lady Butler's 'Floreat Etona' painting hung in every Eton room, and the war chiefs still thought in terms of ponderous British columns in full equipment who had only to appear on the scene in order to scatter a handful of ignorant amateur farmers.

Some British settlers in Pretoria buried a Union Jack in a lavish coffin inscribed 'Resurgam'; but it was Gladstone who made the level-headed comment: 'I have always regarded the South African Question as the one great unsolved and perhaps insoluble problem of our colonial system.'

Kruger's bargaining position had of course been powerfully strengthened by the Boer victories, but he still felt insecure without a seaport. The only suitable way out seemed to be through Portuguese territory, and since both the Portuguese and the Boers needed a railway the Delagoa Bay line was planned, with the Netherlands South Africa

Railway Company floated to construct it. Kruger tried to prevent the British-built Cape and Natal lines from crossing his borders until the Delagoa Bay line was finished, but the Netherlands Company soon became notorious for its incompetence, its jobs for the boys and its general inefficiency: Komati Bridge, for example, in a country abounding in stone, was built of stone imported from Holland, of all places. The cost of the railway, bumped up at every turn by greed for profit and monopoly pressures, added to Transvaal taxes and swelled still further the Outlanders' grievances. There were always more of them to feel the grievances, too: the devil's city grew steadily bigger. The Johannesburg stock exchange opened in June 1887, when so many members crowded the one-storey building and jammed the street outside that an area of pavement had to be permanently reserved for the overspill. It was marked out with iron posts linked by chains, and soon 'between the Chains' was a landmark in the city.

In the autumn of 1894 Rhodes arrived in England at the peak of his prestige, symbol of empire to a country poised between two jubilees, Prime Minister of Cape Colony, responsible for Consolidated Gold Fields Limited, De Beers, the Chartered Company and the new north. Received by the Queen at Windsor and created a Privy Councillor, he stayed at the Burlington Hotel where the suite he occupied cost him £25 a day. Best of all, perhaps, the provinces of Mashonaland and Matabeleland officially became Rhodesia. He was the Lion of Africa, he was Rhodes: Colossus of sorts, and he was just over forty-two years old. John Moffat wrote:

> The great Rhodes is prancing around. The popular tide is with him. Great is success! I wonder the old Greeks and Romans never had a God of Success—that is the sort of god which would be popular nowadays. I suppose there will be a crash some day.

4. The Emigrants' War

'I'll have you know, Mr Rhodes,' said one storekeeper, 'that I did not come here for posterity.'

He was speaking in Rhodesia, where already legends were proliferating about animals which had obligingly dropped dead on the precise spots where gold and copper were subsequently found. Rhodes himself had picked out there the site of his future grave in the Matopos Hills, overlooking what he called the 'World's View', still one of the great sights of Africa. In the opening years of the 1890s, Jameson was fidgeting in Rhodesia and British Bechuanaland, still longing for the daring action that would prove him a worthy disciple of his hero Clive. His chance was now to come, and with it Rhodes' downfall and the emigrants' war.

Stung by Kruger's intractable attitude to the Outlanders into doing something positive, a group of Johannesburg men had started plotting a rising. Among them were an American, John Hays Hammond, and several British, including Rhodes' brother Frank, Lionel Phillips, Charles Leonard, George Farrar and Solly Joel. They smuggled in rifles through the De Beers sidings, hidden under loads of coke or in oil drums with oil dripping convincingly from the taps. Jameson was encouraged to prepare a mounted force and hold it ready in Bechuanaland to move over the border at their signal; he and Beit put up £300,000 to buy arms, rations and horses for the 1,500 men they hoped to recruit. The Chartered Company was constructing the Mafeking–Bulawayo line, and Rhodes persuaded the Colonial Office to grant the Company a strip of land through the Bechuanaland Protectorate for it: down this strip Jameson could come. He soon did so, bringing a posse of Mashonaland Mounted Police and camping them on the Transvaal border as an extra safeguard.

66

Jameson made his own headquarters at Pitsani, about forty miles north of Mafeking, and worked out a code for his messages to and from Johannesburg: the rising was referred to as 'the flotation of company'. But the conspirators ran into all sorts of daft difficulties, one of them a prolonged squabble about the flag they were to march, or rise, under: most of them were happy to keep the Vierkleur flying, but Jameson would not stir except under the Union Jack. Frank Rhodes, who unlike his brother had a reputation as a lady-killer, once agreed to meet Jameson on matters of importance, but when the doctor dashed to Frank's bungalow all he found was a note: 'Dear Jimjams, sorry I can't see you this afternoon, have an appointment to teach Mrs X the bike.' Telegrams buzzed along the wires between Pitsani, Johannesburg and Groote Schuur, where Rhodes was growing more and more uneasy about what he later called 'the fyasco'; once, when someone came to see him, he returned an irritable message to Jameson: 'For God's sake, don't send me any more damned fools like the bearer of this letter.'

As the pretext for the raid, the Reform Committee, as the plotters styled themselves, provided Jameson with an undated letter asking for aid 'should a disturbance arise here':

> Thousands of unarmed men, women and children of our race will be at the mercy of well-armed Boers, while property of enormous value will be in the greatest peril. The circumstances are so extreme that we cannot believe that you and the men under you will not come to the rescue of persons who will be so situated.

This letter was given to Jameson in late November 1895, and zero hour was fixed for 28 December, but right up to the last minute there were nagging doubts. Many of the rifles smuggled in by the Committee were not unpacked by Christmas. Kruger, who had listened with growing anger and a grim smile to the telegraphed messages, moved up to Pretoria where thousands of Boers camped in the Church Square, making capture of the Pretoria arsenal impossible. At this the Committee's nerve, never particularly strong, quailed, and they decided to press for peaceful revolution; Rhodes, vastly relieved, thought the rising had 'fizzled out like a damp squib'.

Jameson, believing that this was all crafty diplomatic camouflage, finished his preparations, and sent a wire: 'Unless I hear definitely to the contrary, shall leave tomorrow evening'. Rhodes in horror wired back: 'On no account whatever must you move. I most strongly object to such a course'. Jameson never got it. He had ordered the telegraph wires cut in order, as he hopefully thought, to ensure secrecy, but not before he had sent a final message to Johannesburg: 'The contractor has started on the earthworks with 700 boys; hopes to reach terminus on Wednesday'. The Committee, reading this on the hot afternoon of 30 December, felt their blood run cold. Frantically they wired 'postpone flotation', but it was too late: Jameson had already crossed the border.

He had paraded his men at Pitsani on Sunday afternoon, 29 December, and read out the Committee's letter, taking care to omit the vital words, 'should a disturbance arise here'. The raiding-party, numbering not the 1,500 he had hoped for, nor even the 700 he said he had, totalled 470 troopers, with a field-gun and two seven-pounders and a few pack-horses. The men carried rations for one day, as Jameson expected to pick up supplies on the way and in any case to reach Johannesburg in fifty hours. At sunset he swung himself on to his black horse and led his column off, wonderful visions of glory filling his mind. No messages, and he received many, could stop him: he simply said that he had to keep faith with his countrymen in their extremity. Rhodes, of course, had in the past made comments like: 'You cannot expect a Prime Minister to write down that you are to seize ports, etc. But when he gives you order to the contrary, disobey them'. By dawn on 30 December Jameson crossed the border, confident of being met by joyful Outlanders cheering their deliverer on New Year's Day.

In Johannesburg the divided Committee, suffering badly from cold feet, made various panicky moves typical of each of them, except for Solly, who stayed calmly playing poker in the Rand Club. John Hays Hammond ran up the Vierkleur on the Consolidated Gold Fields Building, but hoisted it upside down as a defiant gesture. Lionel Phillips began unpacking the rifles. Frank Rhodes sent two cyclists to tell Jameson that an armed detachment would soon be on its way to meet him. Hammond hoped 'the god-damned fool' would break through, but as a precaution sent a wire to the

High Commissioner asking him to protect the lives of his fellow-citizens. Refugees crowded into Pretoria, terrified of being caught in any crossfire, while others streamed out of Johannesburg, cramming the trains bound for Natal, one of which was derailed with considerable loss of life among the women and children on board.

Jameson's hungry and weary cavalcade came on, unaware that they had been virtually abandoned, and equally not knowing that, when their leader ordered the telegraph wires cut, the drunken assistant who performed this office for them had carefully severed the southbound wire to Rhodes but had left intact the eastbound wire to Kruger, who was able to keep perfectly informed about their progress. Rhodes, groaning: 'He has upset my apple cart; Jameson was twenty years my friend and now he has ruined me', restlessly paced the floor at Groote Schuur in agonies of despair and self-reproach, though he rallied sufficiently to send to *The Times* a copy of the fatal letter, thoughtfully dated 28 December by one Rutherfoord Harris. Frank sent out a posse of 120 mounted men under Colonel Bettington, but as the Committee was now trying to negotiate terms with Kruger 'Bettington's Horse' was recalled after galloping only a mile or two. The Chief Justice asked Phillips for proof that the Committee really did represent the Outlanders' views; with incredible naiveté Phillips obligingly wired him the full list of conspirators' names.

With only thirty miles to go, Jameson's men rode straight into the trap at Paardekraal, now renamed Krugersdorp as it was Oom Paul's home town, where 2,000 Boers awaited them with grim relish. Seventy of the tattered invaders were killed or wounded; finally Jameson seized a native woman's white apron and hoisted it in surrender. The column was taken to Pretoria jail, those who could still stand, including their leader, paraded twice round the market square in front of a mocking crowd. 'You may say what you like,' said Jameson doggedly, 'but Clive would have done it.'

Before the full consequences were realized, English reaction was rather admiring: it all seemed like a great lark. Perfectly reflecting the mood was the newly appointed Poet Laureate, Alfred Austin, a diminutive white-moustached producer of dreadful verse whose idea of heaven was to sit in a garden receiving news of British land and sea victories, and who was created Laureate by Lord Salisbury on his normal easy-going principle that one would do as well as another. When friends kindly drew Austin's attention to linguistic errors he replied simply: 'I dare not alter these things. They come to me from above'. Hardly surprisingly, therefore, his first effort as Laureate, published in *The Times* on 11 January 1896, read in part:

> There are girls in the gold-reef city,
> There are mothers and children too!
> And they cry, Hurry up! for pity!
> So what could a brave man do?

> . . . So we forded and galloped forward,
> As hard as our beasts could pelt,
> First eastward, then trending northward,
> Right over the rolling veldt.

> . . . We were wrong, but we aren't half sorry,
> And, as one of the baffled band,
> I would rather have had that foray
> Than the crushings of all the Rand.

The arrested Committee members, even when pelted with stones, mealie cobs and peaches on the way to their trial in Pretoria, stayed quite cheerful. They did not expect anything much to happen to them. Solly Joel's wife Nellie visited him in jail with her hat stuffed with cigars, a bottle of cream in her skirt pocket, and a brace of ducks in her bustle; Natalie Hammond turned up the next day with a large Bologna sausage round her waist. Hammond had another visitor, Mark Twain, who said that a spell in jail provided an excellent rest-cure for a tired business man, but agreed that it was easier to get in than to get out. Barnato cut short a trip to England to rush back and help Solly, saying mournfully: 'How can I face the poor boy's mother if I don't get him out of tronk?'

The Boers were determined that none of the poor boys should get out of tronk. One enthusiast brought along the beam from which the Slagter's Nek rebels had been hanged more than eighty years before; Kruger, unusually smiling, drove through the city in his new state coach, lined with blue silk and bearing the republic's coat of arms on the panels, while the crowds threw flowers at his mounted escort. On Ash Wednesday a train loaded with 2,300 cases of dynamite which had been standing in the sun for three days blew up in a poor suburb of Johannesburg when a shunting engine backed into a truck full of detonators; a hundred people were killed and mutilated and the area was shattered to pieces. The withdrawal of the Company police set off a revolt among the Matabele, who massacred settlers and their families; the Cape Government sent troops under General Carrington to restore order. Rhodes went along, determined to save his cherished territory, taking the unofficial rank of colonel. In his white flannels, Norfolk jacket and slouch hat he fought with what Mr Gardner called 'a kind of crazed gallantry'. Carrington's Chief of Staff was a trim, sunburnt officer with a fair moustache and twinkling eyes whose name was Robert Stephenson Smyth Baden-Powell.

The trial of the sixty-four prisoners was quick and ended with brutal sentences: the death penalty for Hammond, Farrar, Phillips, and Frank Rhodes; two years' imprisonment, three years' banishment and £2,000 fines for the rest. Jameson had been sent back for trial in England, where he was given the lightest possible sentence—fifteen months— of which he served four. Barnato went to see Kruger and threatened to close down his business if the death sentences were carried out. He meant it; it would have ruined the Transvaal, and Kruger gave in, commuting the sentences to fines only, except for the leaders, whose fines were set at £25,000 each plus a choice of banishment or promising to stay inactive in local affairs for fifteen years. Frank Rhodes chose exile, and was escorted to the border that evening, 30 May, by armed Boers. Rhodes paid all the fines at once. The raid cost him about £800,000.

It cost him more than that. He felt obliged to resign as Cape Prime Minister and as head of the Chartered Company. The crash, predicted by Moffat, had come; the years of glory were over.

H. M. Hole, Jameson's secretary, wrote that he was

> unversed in official routine, impatient of formality and always prone to take short cuts to achieve his purpose —defects which were nevertheless an advantage in enabling him to deal expeditiously with the daily problems of the Pioneer community.

And Mr A. J. Hanna points out that if the raid had succeeded Jameson would have been the British Garibaldi;
'this gifted and gallant man . . . [of] frankness, charm, and
buoyancy of spirit' is mainly remembered because of the
'fyasco' rather than for all the rest of his considerable and
creditable work.

There were other consequences of the raid, some immedi-
ately harsh, others not at first clear. The newly appointed
Transvaal State Attorney renounced his British nationality
in disgust. He was a young Cape lawyer, Jan Christiaan
Smuts, later to be second Prime Minister of the Union and
described by Mr John Gunther as a soldier, statesman,
philosopher 'of the most lofty elevation . . . his mind coiled,
thin, and tightly strung like the mainspring of a watch';
carrying copies of Kant, Tacitus and the Greek New Testament in his saddlebags on early campaigns, walking for
hours on Table Mountain in middle life; caring nothing for
money or display, his first book an essay on Whitman,
planning a league of nations before Woodrow Wilson did,
helping to form the Versailles Treaty and the United
Nations, inventor of the term 'Commonwealth'—this was
his first, deceptively unassuming, appearance on the international scene.

All over Southern Africa, British and Afrikaner drew
apart. Fear, recriminations, broken friendships, bitter mistrust corroded the relationships of years. What the affronted
Boers saw as treachery became part of a pattern of deception
that ran back over years of dispute, poisoning past dealings.
The British in their turn were outraged by a warmly con-
gratulatory telegram from the German Emperor to Kruger:
this deepened the Anglo-German rifts as well as the Anglo-
Boer. The Orange Free State drew away from the Cape and
closer to the Transvaal, where Kruger was triumphantly re-
elected for a fourth term. Stronger than ever in his burghers'
esteem and his enhanced prestige over the Jameson affair,
he pressed harder than before against the Outlanders' franchise. Queen Victoria assured her daughter Vicky, the
Kaiser's mother, that the Boers were 'horrid people, cruel
and overbearing' and that Jameson was 'an excellent and
able man'. Suspicions of complicity in the raid of highly
placed Britons, particularly Colonial Secretary Joseph
Chamberlain, crystallized among the Afrikaners, though

proof that the plans had involved him did not emerge for over half a century.

From 1897 on, both sides—for that is what they now were —began to prepare for open conflict. That was the year of the Diamond Jubilee, when outwardly Britain was at the peak of imperial glory. Splendid troops from all parts of the Empire, somewhat pompously referred to as 'the lion's cubs', filled the great procession to St Paul's, bringing the little old Queen in her carriage to the thanksgiving service celebrating the glittering height of prestige. One person who had expected to be present was not: Barnato, sailing to England on the crack liner *Scot*, inexplicably went overboard on Monday, 14 June 1897. By the time they pulled him out of the water, he was dead, and an unresolved did-he-fall-or-was-he-pushed question has clung to his death ever since: a spectacular end to a spectacular life.

At the very moment of the Jubilee, one warning voice was heard: that of a thirty-six year old writer of stories and poems who had already commented on South Africa in his 'Hymn Before Action' and a set of four stanzas inspired by Jameson and called 'If': Rudyard Kipling, who now produced 'Recessional', with its lines, truer perhaps than he knew:

> Lo, all our pomp of yesterday
> Is one with Nineveh and Tyre!

This was not yet apparent to the general view. Britain still looked like the world colossus, hated, envied, admired as all world superpowers are in their turn. An anonymous settler put something of this feeling into a scornful parody:

> God save our gracious foes,
> Long live our noble foes,
> God save our foes.
> Send them victorious,
> Long to laugh over us,
> Always pro-Boer-ious,
> God save our foes.
>
> May we be always meek,
> Turning the other cheek,
> Though it should hurt.
> Confound Chamberlain Joe,

The British to Southern Africa

Frustrate John Bull and Co.,
Bring Empire-builders low,
Make them eat dirt.

May every nation thrive,
Plan, scheme, lie, threat and strive,
While we give way.
This be our lofty tone,
Long live each land and throne,
Except, of course, our own—
Hoo blooming ray!

Chamberlain, alarmed by reports of massive arms-stock-piling in the Transvaal, and unable to decide whether Kruger was preparing to see reason or simply biding his time, appointed Sir Alfred Milner, 'the finest flower of culture that had been reared in the University [Oxford] of that generation', later described as 'the Prussian tax-collector' because he had been educated in Germany and had headed the Inland Revenue, as High Commissioner to South Africa in 1898 Milner was stiff-necked and chilly, but learned to read the Afrikaner newspapers and realized the mistrust and resentment running so deeply on both sides. 'There is no way out' he concluded within a few months, 'except reform in the Transvaal or war'.

The Outlanders drew up another petition, stating once again the understandable grievances of those who virtually created the wealth of the Transvaal and paid most of its taxes yet were not permitted to belong, and, tired of submitting the old requests to the unrelenting Kruger, sent it to Queen Victoria in April 1899. Chamberlain, to whom the Queen passed it for action, drafted an acceptance acknowledging the justice of the Outlanders' complaints, and meanwhile asked Milner's opinion. Milner promptly sent back an inflammatory declaration stating that 'the case for intervention is overwhelming' to set right the lowering spectacle of 'thousands of British subjects kept permanently in the position of helots', and offering to meet Kruger personally to try for a summit settlement.

The Bloemfontein Conference, as their meeting was known, opened on Wednesday 31 May, and speedily demonstrated the clash of the irresistible force with the immovable object. Milner commented bitterly on the Boers 'eternal

War in the Transvaal: flight of the inhabitants from Johannesburg, 1896

duplicity'; Kruger angrily (and accurately) exclaimed: 'It is our country you want!' The Conference broke off in deadlock, war scares spread, the press released the 'helots' despatch, and the jingo element in England scented blood. So did the Opposition, until the more reasonable among them were stopped dead in their tracks somewhat surprisingly by the ironic voice of Henrik Ibsen, asking with calm logic: 'Are we really on the side of Kruger and his Old Testament?' German and Dutch weapons poured into Afrikaner arsenals, General Sir Redvers Buller became Commander-in-Chief with the spacious comment that he knew everything about South Africa, the Australians offered troops and were solemnly told that unmounted men were preferred, and Rhodes wrote in September:

> If Kruger does not climb down, the New Year will see us masters of Pretoria. I don't understand how you can trouble yourself about the matter. You would not care if you heard there was a quarrel between your cook and her kitchenmaid. This business has no importance whatever.

The recipient of this letter was Princess Catherine Radziwill, a charming, cultivated and witty divorcee of forty-seven, who was determined to marry Rhodes; she sailed when he did on the *Dunottar Castle* in July, finding Jameson at the Cape to meet the ship, by which time the Princess had a standing invitation to Groote Schuur, but no proposal.

As the messages batted back and forth between London and Pretoria and Milner considered that Kruger would 'bluff up to the cannon's mouth', those who were to have particular effect on the shape of things to come were beginning to assemble. One of the most colourful was General Sir Charles Warren, an irritable official in his late fifties, who had surveyed the Orange Free State boundary, settled the Bechuanaland Protectorate (where he made a balloon ascent), surveyed the Rock of Gibraltar and the archaeology of Palestine, served as OC Straits Settlements, and had recently completed three years as Commissioner of the Metropolitan Police (Buller crossly called him 'this dug-out ex-policeman'). In all these posts he had succeeded in giving offence to many, and in the last had been responsible for

'Bloody Sunday' in Trafalgar Square. He had also failed to capture Jack the Ripper. He had a habit of dropping, perhaps unconsciously, into verse when drafting orders: one of these read: 'The Commissioner has observed there are signs of wear on the Landseer Lions in Trafalgar Square. Unauthorized persons are not to climb on the Landseer Lions at any time'. Buller, who had learned to dread Warren's fulminating despatches from Singapore, now found that Warren had been appointed by Wolseley as Buller's second-in-command, to take over if his chief were 'killed or bowler-hatted'.

Buller himself, now sixty, did not escape criticism. His forty years of Army service, his legendary courage, and his unfailing solicitude for his men's comfort, were insufficient protection against comments like Churchill's: 'He plodded on from blunder to blunder and from one disaster to another, without losing either the regard of his country or the trust of his troops'; Mr Martin's 'a bumbling general of the old British school, stocky, red-faced, and under-exercised —with no knowledge of the region, the people or the psychology of the Boers'; or Ian Hamilton's 'a red-faced Martian devoid of common sense . . . I doubt if a man who has been filling his belly with all manner of good things for over ten years in the neighbourhood of Pall Mall can ever quite rise to the rough and tumble of a big command with a formidable enemy'; 'he only thinks of his cooks and fleshpots: he ought to be pensioned'. Certainly Buller had luxurious quarters in the field: Dr Ransford refers to 'a superb tent, an iron bathroom, and a sumptuous kitchen' and 'his pint of champagne every day during the campaign, and very good champagne too'. The only privation was apparently 'an occasional lack of butter'.

Kruger's ultimatum, asking the British to withdraw all their troops from the Transvaal, was rejected, and war was then certain. The Outlanders began moving out, packing the trains to Natal. Boer commandos came out of the veld and converged on Pretoria. Kipling flung in his contribution:

> When you've shouted 'Rule Britannia', when you've
> sung 'God save the Queen',
> When you've finished killing Kruger with your mouth,
>
> Will you kindly drop a shilling in my little tambourine
> For a gentleman in khaki ordered South?

The British to Southern Africa

Duke's son—cook's son—son of a hundred kings—
(Fifty thousand horse and foot going to Table Bay!) . . .

and all over Southern Africa the British forces already on
the spot stood to their arms. Sometimes these were laughably
few: on the Rhodesian frontier Colonel Plumer's thirty
policemen were all that stood in the path of the Boers. The
ultimatum ran out at 5 p.m. on 11 October; three days later,
Buller sailed on the *Dunottar Castle*, seen off by crowds
shouting 'Remember Majuba!' and commanding an army
twice the size of any that had served under Marlborough or
Wellington. On board also was a war correspondent recom-
mended by Chamberlain to Milner as

> a very clever young fellow with many of his father's
> qualifications. He has the reputation of being bump-
> tious, but I have not myself found him so.

This was Winston Churchill, drawn as always by the magnet
of a fight. He observed the 'trance-like' calm of the voyage,
cut off from news for twelve days, so that he like the rest
was unaware of the first engagements. The Boers crossed the
Natal frontier under black clouds scattering snow at (of all
places) Laing's Nek, and moved to attack General Penn
Symons at Talana, south of Newcastle. On the way they
captured Elandslaagte, cutting off the road to Ladysmith,
and stationed themselves on the Talana slopes in the wet
dawn mist of 20 October. Penn Symons brushed his long
moustaches and scanty brown hair, fastened his high gold-
braided collar and was ready for battle, the mist rose at 5.30
and the Boer gunners, amid applause, sent the war's first
shell screeching over the troops' heads, and by nightfall
Penn Symons and 546 others were dead or wounded, while
the Boers, with 150 casualties, had possession of Dundee's
water supply.

The war rapidly split into two categories, battle and
siege. Three towns were bottled up: Ladysmith, Kimberley
and Mafeking. The battles, on the part of the British a
sequence of ludicrous and famous fumbles, culminated in
the triple disasters of Black Week in December, in which
General Gatacre at Stormberg, Lord Methuen at Magersfontein, and Buller himself at Colenso on the Tugela, were
all, incredibly, defeated. Among the dead at Colenso was a

young Lieutenant Roberts, whose father, a professional soldier, was shortly to arrive in South Africa.

As our principal concern here is with the British settlers, their reactions to the war can best be seen by looking at the three sieges rather than at the separate battles, for many immigrants found themselves spending stretches of time in one of the invested places.

Dr James Alexander Kay, born in Plymouth in 1849, son of a Naval surgeon, had left the University of Aberdeen to spend ten years as doctor on an Antarctic whaler. Refuelling at Durban in 1879, Kay joined the RAMC in the Zulu War, and then was stationed in Pretoria during the Transvaal occupation. He left after Majuba, but came back after marrying Alice, daughter of General William Ashburner of the Bombay Lancers, and set up his practice in the capital. Nineteen years' residence had not altered his British sympathies: throughout 1899 he regularly sent information to the British authorities, and enjoyed working out a possible code using the numbers on banknotes. Finding himself under the scrutiny of the Boers, he sent his wife and children to Natal and subsequently followed them disguised as a woman, having shaved off his moustache and set a blonde wig on his bald head. The Natal Government accepted his services and sent him to Ladysmith, where he kept a lively diary and wrote despatches that eventually got him accredited as war correspondent to *The Western Morning News*.

Ladysmith was two main streets and had 4,500 civilians hoping to shelter under the protection of the troops commanded by Sir George White, a sixty-five year old Irish professional soldier with a rather undistinguished career. Neither he nor his opponent, Piet Joubert, who was the same age, really came to grips; White was determined to sit out the siege waiting for Buller's relief force, but he was going to have to wait a long time. There were more casualties from disease than from shot or shell, and football matches and mule races enlivened the boredom: one day a shell fell in the middle of the pitch during a match, but the soldiers filled in the crater and went on playing. Colonel R. W. Mapleton, principal Medical Officer of the Infantry Division, commented on the comparatively little damage most of the shells caused, that the town was in touch with Buller by heliograph 'but he tells us very little', and added:

We get lots to eat though I dare say you would turn up your snout at it, for the quality though all right for camp is not what one would select for choice, still besieged people have to be thankful for what they can get. The water is like pea soup but we boil it and filter it ... I have seen some of the Boers ... very pleasant fellows indeed and very friendly. They have behaved *extremely* well to our wounded prisoners, attending to them and giving them everything they had themselves.

Perturbed at finding Ladysmith swarming with spies, Dr Kay alerted the Intelligence Department on 25 October, and received the reply that 'one more or less makes no difference', causing him to write irritably: 'Beyond censoring letters, interrogating prisoners, and purloining all newspapers and cigarettes brought in by private runners, no one knows what Intelligence does'; a little later he added: 'It does nothing, knows nothing and pays nothing'. Of the Boer Long Tom gun he wrote cheerfully that it was 'a matchless advertisement for its French factory, for despite firing steadily all day it did little or no damage. We have christened it "Puffing Billy".' He put messages in bottles and threw them in the river; they read that 'all were well and jolly', 'animal spirits good, liquid spirits scarce, food plentiful'. But he wrote to Alice:

Ladysmith is an awful hole, celebrated for heat, dust storms, wind and insects. Scorpions and tarantulas are larger here than any I have seen before ... There are so many yarns knocking about that one can't believe anything. Nearly everyone in this camp is a liar or a thief —many are both. If you leave a bucket outside your tent for a minute it is gone.

The doctor himself succumbed, not without relish.

Matches are very scarce and candles are unobtainable. I received a visit from a friend, and directly he left I missed a box with nine matches in it; they were all I had. I accused him of taking them but he denied it most indignantly ... I had to be satisfied with his denial. I must confess that a few days later I stole from him a milk tin full of candle droppings ... I think I scored.

On the road to the front: 'Curry's Post' (from a sketch by Melton Prior)

The British to Southern Africa

This was my only theft but shortly afterwards my water-proof was stolen and I was rightly punished.

Christmas Day was enlivened by the Boers firing in two shells stuffed with Christmas pudding with the words 'A Merry Xmas' painted on the casing; a curio-hunter bought one for fifteen pounds. At seven in the evening a children's party was held in a large room at the back of the Standard Bank, decorated by (among others) Frank Rhodes, with four Christmas trees labelled Britain, Australia, Canada, South Africa; there was plenty of cake and lemonade, and Dr Kay enjoyed a whisky and soda. He went on to a dinner party that would have sat down thirteen at table if somebody had not hurriedly sent out and found a petty officer to join them in consuming very good soup, turkey, sucking-pig, pudding, sherry, Black Velvet, and whisky 'ad lib' in which they toasted 'Her Most Gracious Majesty the Queen' and 'To Hell with the Boers'. The party broke up at five in the morning.

In January 1900 Dr Kay reported:

The Boers are building a dam of sandbags on the Klip River. A small engine and trucks bring the bags; British guns at Caesar's Camp fire at it but don't hit. The train dodges about with impunity along the curves of the line, half hidden by the bushes. Barely more than half a mile from our camp, it affords us endless interest watching the shots.

In February he was noting the sky-high prices of goods, seventeen shillings for a tin of coffee, forty-eight for a dozen eggs, eighteen for 'a plate of tomatoes', thirty for a pound of marmalade, twenty-five for a packet of cigarettes and thirteen and six for a dozen boxes of matches. He paid seven pounds for a bottle of whisky and five for four tins of milk. At this time he noted the temperature in his tent registered 116 'with an accurate thermometer'. One day he met a British patrol and was appalled at their weight of equipment; 'Every man and every horse was decked out like a Christmas tree' (the identical phrase used by Colonel Spencer Chapman in Malaya forty-one years and two wars later). 'Why any man', fumed the doctor, 'should carry more than his rifle and ammunition into battle, a haversack and a blanket, is what all would like to know'. He shared Churchill's opinion that armoured trains were unwieldy traps, and on one of his Pietermaritzburg trips sadly noted the damage the fighting had done to formerly prosperous farmland. In late August, 2,000 Transvaal stamps marked VRI were issued at five shillings each; within two weeks they fetched fifteen, and old sets of stamps between fifteen and twenty pounds. There was also a flourishing market for coins: a Transvaal penny was 'cheap at one and six', while five-shilling pieces with 'double shafts to the wagon' brought seven pounds ten.

At about the same time a friend sent Dr Kay a poster that was appearing on the streets of Cape Town:

THEATRE ROYAL

The management beg to notify the public that they have secured the services of several of our generals, and some notorious artists to take part in a variety show, the proceeds to be given to the few survivors of the starving refugees. The recognition and sufferings of these deserving and ruined creatures should appeal to all.

Programme

1 An address on 'The instruction of idiots for military purposes' by General de Wet, formerly of the Boer Army, now instructor of strategy and military tactics, Staff College.
2 A lecture on 'Magnanimity and How to Fight with Kid Gloves' by Field Marshal Lord Roberts (Bobs).
3 A lecture on 'Automatic Incubators and Egg-Hatching' by General Buller (Sitting Bull).
4 Song: 'There's Life in the Old Dog Yet' by Ex-President Kruger.
5 Discussion: 'What Not to do in War and How to Do It' by the Entire Staff of the Staff College.

God Save the Queen

Eventually Dr Kay was sent to a tent hospital two miles out of Pretoria on the Middelburg road, where the 'streets' of tents were marked out with geometrically accurate lines of whitewashed stones and even the tent-pegs precisely aligned on the clean, tidy grounds; the water supply was 'absolutely perfect', ample and excellent. Nearby were two other hospitals, the Welsh (which had a French chef imported from the Hotel Cecil) and the Langman. In all three 'patients could not possibly be better cared for in the heart of London'.

After months of blundering about, Buller finally hauled his huge, cumbersome columns on to the last miles of the road to Ladysmith, and brought the 118-day siege to an end on 28 February 1900. It had been a shattering ordeal for the Army: losing 1,127 casualties at Colenso without seeing a live Boer, still less a dead one; for Warren, reporting in a bad temper on Boxing Day at Buller's HQ at Frere; for Buller himself, sitting apparently impassively on his big bay horse and hearing of the scornful Boer signals: 'What has Mr Buller done that Roberts is coming out?' and trying to get 650 ox-wagons across streams turned into torrents by the rain. One day the Waschbank was three inches deep; by nightfall it was twelve feet, and thirty-five yards wide. The Army had moved at a crawl, stretched over fifteen miles and taking thirteen hours to pass a given point, yet maddeningly able to see the sun glinting on the roofs of Ladysmith eighteen miles away, when they came to Spion Kop where 5,000 British soldiers were a dream target to 600 Boers. What Dr Ransford called 'the deadliest fighting in South African history' was watched in agonized helplessness by thousands of troops, including Buller on Spearman's Hill where doves cooed in the trees. Of the trapped British on the summit, nobody broke, nobody ran, everybody who died, died hard: it was said that ever after the yellowed grass on Spion Kop has shown red-tinged after frost. Hardly had the smoke begun to blow away when the recriminations began; it was Majuba's carbon copy.

Over in Kimberley, across the wide plain with its humble little rivers and low hills at Belmont and Magersfontein, another doctor was keeping a journal. This was Dr Oliver Ashe, whose angry, spluttering notes were later expanded into a book. He, like Mapleton, felt keenly the lack of hard news:

> We don't want to know what are the plans of the general, but we can't help wanting to know something of the things that have happened. I suppose the army red tape forbids anything being told civilians until it is

too old to interest them. And the folly of that red tape!
Oh, Lord, how silly it is!

By far the unhappiest man in Kimberley was Lieutenant-
Colonel Robert George Kekewich of the Loyal North Lancashire Regiment, who was Commander-in-Chief of the town's
defences. Other places simply had the Boers in their *laagers*
outside; he had Rhodes on the spot. In early December
Methuen sent to Kekewich:

> Please understand that I can give you 1½ battalions and
> naval brigade, and you must cut your coat according to
> your cloth. I am arranging military defence with you,
> and Rhodes must understand that he has no voice in
> the matter.

Rhodes, of course, was furious at this, and proved to be
a thorny problem, giving orders and sending despatches over
Kekewich's head, indignantly criticizing Kekewich and
everybody else, and infuriatingly making himself indispens-
able by supplying shells (inscribed 'Compliments CJR')
produced by the American Chief Mechanical Engineer of
De Beers, George Labram. The Boer shells were no more
impressive in Kimberley than they had been in Ladysmith;
after bombardments there was a rush to pick up pieces as
souvenirs, the bottom of a shell and its conical point being
especially sought-after. Lawsuits were actually threatened to
settle the ownership of bits of shell.

Methuen was more active than Buller, and his troops were
reinforced by volunteers from Queensland, Toronto, Ire-
land and Cornwall, but he soon found that nothing could
move near the Modder River without raising clouds of white
dust. However, a new couple came on the scene: the supreme
command of the British Army in South Africa was given to
its most famous soldier, Field-Marshal Lord Roberts of
Kandahar, 'a little red-faced man, rides the tallest 'orse 'e
can' (an Arab grey, Vonolel), and known throughout the
Army simply as 'Bobs'. With him arrived his massive square-
faced inscrutable second, Kitchener of Khartoum, 'K'. Other
famous names, entering history for the first time in the Boer
War, included John Denton Pinkstone French, commanding
the cavalry, and his Chief of Staff, Douglas Haig. Between
them they managed to relieve Kimberley on 15 February,

two weeks earlier than Ladysmith, and went on to force Piet Cronje to surrender at Paardeburg. The *Daily Mail's* report showed the priorities of the period:

> Kimberley is won, Mr Cecil Rhodes is free, the De Beers shareholders are all full of themselves, and the beginning of the war is at an end. It is a great feat to have accomplished, and the happiest omen for the future. There is no one like Bobs!

The third siege was the most celebrated, and certainly in retrospect the most comic: Mafeking.

'Just a small tin-roofed town of small houses plumped down upon the open veldt' is how Baden-Powell described it: above all else it was isolated, 420 miles south-west of Bulawayo, 200 miles north of Kimberley. Its buildings were constructed of earthy sand and mud that could be powdered in the hand and upon which shells made no impression save a hole in passing through. The shells came from the big 94-pounder nicknamed 'Creaky' by the British, for it could be heard (and seen) being laid on its target, and there was always plenty of time to give the alarm and to take cover.

Probably the real hero of Mafeking was the local contractor, Benjamin Weil, who accepted on no very secure grounds a note of hand for half a million pounds from Major Lord Edward Cecil, Baden-Powell's Chief of Staff, and spent the money on an incredible variety and quantity of supplies, filling his apparently bottomless stores and preventing the besieged from feeling any of the privations suffered in the other two invested towns. Whereas Rhodes provided Kimberley with Christmas puddings and Dr Ashe wrote that it was 'very funny to see all the town's big swells either fetching their meat themselves or sending a member of their family for it', the happy residents of Mafeking sat down to a nine-course Christmas dinner in Riesle's Hotel, all of it from Weil's stores, which were still only one-third used up. Mafeking had style, in its way, too: Lady Sarah Wilson, daughter of the Duke of Marlborough and a first-rate nuisance when she wanted to be, had constructed a delightful bombproof shelter, white-panelled and cool, with an excellent bed, dressing-table, and hot-line telephone to Baden-Powell's headquarters; Lord Charles Cavendish-Bentinck, commanding a cavalry squadron, passed the Mafeking

Mafeking Siege one-pound note, designed by Baden-Powell

armoured train and shouted: 'Go along and engage them, and when you find them, give them beans'; Baden-Powell sent out (by the regular runners) despatches saying things like 'Killed: 1 hen; wounded: 1 yellow dog; smashed: 1 window' in the intervals of digging trenches and dug-outs, spending hours whistling as he watched the Boers through his field-glasses, encouraging the making of searchlights out of biscuit-tins, and, above all, arranging endless programmes of social and sporting events, particularly on Sundays, when the Boers would not fire or fight. Mr Gardner says in his enchanting account that 'Often he seemed more like the host at some huge, jolly party than a military commander'. Although he did everything but bring his forces and the enemy to anything approaching a full-scale confrontation, and controversy has raged ever since about the value of the siege as holding large Boer groups immobile or even whether those were his original orders, there is no doubt that the huge prestige Mafeking gave him enabled him to confer on the world the benefits of the Scout movement, and that he sensed the opportunity from the beginning: 'he looked like a man having the time of his life, and, indeed, there is every indication that he was'. Back in England, a siege was a siege, and the jolly messages out of Mafeking were taken as supreme examples of the Colonel's pluck, which helps to explain why he was so idolized afterwards, and why the name of his town passed into the English language to indicate wild outbursts of civilian jubilation.

As the post went in and out (not a feature of most sieges), Rhodes wrote to Lady Sarah: 'Just a line to say I often think of you. We play bridge every evening. I wonder do you; it takes your mind off hospital, burials and shells'. Several war correspondents, 'the cream of their profession', were in Mafeking; perhaps the most interesting of these was Emerson Neilly of *The Pall Mall Gazette*, who frequently rode out to talk to the Boers and returned to dine and smoke cigars at the hotel before writing up his lively reports. Long stretches of time were boring, but there was little tense anticipation of the relief, now being organized on Roberts's orders by Major Baden Baden-Powell, one of B-P's brothers, at Barkly West. The column, led by Colonel Bryan Mahon, featured the famous Imperial Light Horse, which had been first in at Ladysmith and wanted to do it again at Mafeking.

Frank Rhodes was going, too: had not Jameson based his raid in the beleaguered town? When Baden-Powell asked for details of the relief force, Frank Rhodes worked out the code:

> Our numbers are Naval and Military Club multiplied by ten; our guns, the number of sons in the Ward family; our supplies, the OC 9th Lancers.

This was easy—the Club was at 94 Piccadilly, which meant 940 men; the Earl of Dudley and his five brothers were the Ward sons, which meant six guns; and the OC was Lieutenant-Colonel Little, so supplies were few. No matter: the column made the 250-mile march in twelve days, arriving on 17 May 1900. The Imperial Light Horse were first in, but were disconcerted to find that the townspeople had preferred watching the final of the billiards tournament to waiting breathlessly for the relief to appear. Major Davies, who led the cavalry, told a passer-by who he was. 'Oh, yes,' answered the man calmly. 'I heard you were knocking about'. It was left to the British, 7,000 miles away in England, to go wild at the news: and they did.

On 28 May, Roberts proclaimed the annexation of the Orange Free State; on 5 June he entered Pretoria (where the buried Union Jack was exhumed and hoisted); and in November he returned to a hero's welcome in England, leaving Kitchener to mop up, a long, slow operation involving eighteen months' guerrilla warfare, with all the notorious drives, block-houses, concentration camps (the first use of this ill-starred name) and lasting resentment on the part of the Boers. There were lighter moments: from Concordia on 28 April 1902 one S. G. Maritz addressed a letter to 'The Hon. Major Edwards' asking for a rugby match: 'I, from my side, will agree to a cease-fire tomorrow afternoon from 12 o'clock until sunset, the time and venue of the match to be arranged by you in consultation with Messrs Roberts and Van Rooyen who I am sending to you'. But the war ended, technically, on 31 May 1902 with the peace treaty signed at Vereeniging. Its terms were generous: Kipling, who had praised the Boer fighting quality ('I ain't more proud of 'avin' won Than I am pleased with Piet'), summed it up:

The British to Southern Africa

Ah, there, Piet! with your brand-new English plough,
Your gratis tents an' cattle, an' your most ungrateful
frow,
You've made the British taxpayer rebuild your country-
seat—
I've known some pet battalions charge a dam' sight less
than Piet.

But others put it differently, although they meant the same:
Britain had won the war, but the Boers had won the
country. One need only look at the list of Union Prime
Ministers to see that—General Louis Botha, General Jan
Smuts, General James Barry Munnik Hertzog, Dr Daniel
François Malan, Johannes Gerhardus Strijdom, Dr Hendrik
Frensch Verwoerd, Balthazar Johannes Vorster.

The old protagonists went home: Buller to grow apples in
Devon, Lord Dundonald, who had fought at Spion Kop, to
invent the naval smokescreen, and Warren, who at the same
battle had been so annoyed by young Mr Churchill that he
had snapped: 'Who is this man? Take him away. Put him in
arrest', withdrew to Kent and wrote about weights and
measures, ran a Sunday school class in Ramsgate, raised the
first Ramsgate scout troop and ended up as a dear old man
loved by everybody until he died in 1927 aged eighty-six.
The younger ones looked to their prospects and prepared
for glittering triumphs in the next war—Hamilton, Smith-
Dorrien, Plumer, French, Haig. Twenty-three veterans of
Spion Kop turned up there for a memorial service in 1964.

Rhodes did not live to see Vereeniging. His premonition
had been right. He did not hope for paradise: 'I don't believe in the idea about going to heaven and twanging a harp
all day', he had said, though he also declared that he was
not an atheist. In his last illness he lapsed into semi-con-
sciousness, rambling through long conversations with God,
in which he spoke for both God and himself. The old
Southern Africa was dying indeed.

5. The Old Imperials

'Here lie the remains of Cecil John Rhodes'. This laconic inscription marks the grave at the 'World's View', where Mr Gunther found a vast slippery black rock carpeted with 'chartreuse, lemon and reddish green' lichens bearing scars made by the gun-carriage when the coffin was lugged laboriously up: 'Rhodes left his imprint even on rock'. He died on 26 March 1907, leaving a legacy as mixed as his character had been: his name indelibly on the map, where he had added 800,000 square miles to Britain's territories, the money that he never cared for enriching the cause of university scholarship, his imperial dream unrealized but beckoning others to follow it, and his legend, incorporating such incongruities as his hatred of trippers' litter on the slopes of Table Mountain and his loving bequest of Groote Schuur as the Chequers of his adopted country. His body lay in state in Cape Town cathedral; after the funeral service it travelled by train to Bulawayo, watched all along the 750-mile route by mourning crowds and saluted at blockhouses by troops knowing that even the track they guarded was a product of his vision. He left an estimated fortune of between twenty-five and forty-five million pounds and the belief that his name would be remembered for four thousand years. His grave is at one of the world's most starkly impressive resting-places—alongside (the last incongruity) that of Jameson, who outlived him by exactly fifteen years and eight months.

The Boers did not take easily to the idea of stopping the fighting, which is why the guerrilla warfare and the mopping-up took so long. Dissensions split the leaders: in January 1901 Botha told Pretorius: 'Tell Kruger we don't want messages and we don't want peace. It is he that wants peace. We want our independence and we will fight till we get it.

91

Tell him he has the railways but we have the country'. It was this attitude that held the Afrikaners so that in the end there was nothing for it but the Union.

Kruger went into exile, dying in Switzerland in 1904, while the British dealt with the aftermath as best they knew how. To help in the tidying-up and administration, Milner imported a group of brilliant young men known as 'Milner's Kindergarten' who included such future celebrities as Geoffrey Dawson, Patrick Duncan, Philip Kerr, and, above all, John Buchan. Anyone who wants to find the genuine flavour of English governmental opinion concerning South Africa in the opening years of the present century can hardly do better than read *Prester John*, published in 1910. In it the storyteller praises the Afrikaners and remarks, of his conversation with the native chief, Laputa:

> I blush today to think of the stuff I talked. First I made him sit on a chair opposite me, a thing no white man in the country would have done. Then I told him affectionately that I liked natives, that they were fine fellows and better men than the dirty whites round about. I explained that I was fresh from England, and believed in equal rights for all men, white or coloured. God forgive me, but I think I said I hoped to see the day when Africa would belong once more to its rightful masters.

Buchan obviously fell under the spell of Southern Africa: not for nothing is his most famous character, Richard Hannay, a Rhodesian; but Milner never did. 'I have always been unfortunate in disliking my life and surroundings here.' For this reason he failed. His decision to import Chinese labour for the mines helped to defeat his party in 1906, and his efforts to anglicize South Africa stiffened Afrikaner opposition, predictably enough. Gradually it became clear even to the blindest that the only answer was Union, and one of the architects of Union was the Cape Prime Minister of 1904–1908, our old acquaintance Dr Jameson.

One small but infallible sign that South Africa was a country in its own right appeared in 1906, when on 27 August the first South Africa touring rugby team sailed on the Union Castle liner *Gascon* for England. The *Daily Mail* of 20 September explained:

The Old Imperials

The team's colours will be myrtle green jerseys with gold collar. They will wear dark blue shorts and dark blue stockings, and the jerseys will have embroidered in mouse-coloured silk on the left breast a springbok, a small African antelope which is as typical of Africa as the kangaroo is of Australia.

The team arranged among themselves to call themselves Springboks, with the disarming comment: 'The witty London press would invent some funny name for us if we did not invent one ourselves.'

In 1905 a man called Wells dug out with his penknife a diamond the size of a fist. It took three men eight months, working fourteen hours a day, to cut it into nine large stones and ninety-six brilliants. The first, the vital cut, achieved after weeks of nervous study and experiment, had so strung-up the cutter, Mr Asscher, that, as the great diamond fell into its two pieces in precisely the right way on 10 February 1908, he fainted. The two principal jewels taken from the original can be seen today in the British crown and sceptre. The diamond was the Cullinan.

There were, occasionally, pink, yellow, and blue diamonds, and some found near gold had a green tinge, but the majority were, as they still are, the true watery blue-white impossible to copy. In addition to the diamonds and the gold, there is the vital uranium, also chrome, manganese, copper, lead, zinc, asbestos and coal: all solid props for any country's economy. For years people worried in case the veins gave out. Recent discoveries of gold in the Orange Free State and diamonds in South-West Africa show that these gloomy forebodings are needless for a long time yet.

By the act of Union in 1910 the four provinces were federated into one entity, and from then on the country has divided into a clear-cut dualism of authority, on the one hand the Afrikaner, focusing more and more upon the Nationalist Party which has split from time to time and invariably to the right politically, and on the other the great trusts and combines that control the minerals. This dualism really reflects the Boer versus Briton pattern. Even the Union flag sketches the immigration movements; flags, 'the shorthand of history', merit a glance in this connexion. The tricolour of orange, white, and blue, deriving from the Prinsevlag of William of Orange, carries three small flags in its white stripe, the Union Jack, the flag of the Orange Free State hanging vertically (seven white and orange stripes with a small Netherlands tricolour in the canton), and the Vierkleur of the Transvaal. The pale blue Air Force ensign has the national flag in the canton and, on the fly, a leaping springbok on a stylized plan of Cape Town Castle.

Rhodesia opened up a good deal later than the Union itself. In spite of Rhodes, in spite of the Pioneers, settlement there was slow and scattered until astonishingly late—right into the twenties people were coming in to live in their own hand-built grass houses; miles of land for the asking existed far past the time when estate-agents were tightening their grip on South Africa. As in the original colony, settlers trickled rather than streamed, finding a do-it-yourself territory of idyllic primitiveness. But just as the Outlanders had struggled against Kruger's government, so the early British in Rhodesia fought the Chartered Company for land rights and for political representation. In 1903 the Legislative Council had seven elected members and seven Company officials; by 1914 it was twelve to two. The Company originally said that it owned all the land not yet occupied, and it was this that the settlers fought, though, as Mr Hanna points out, when the Company invested its capital in the economy 'they were content to milk the Chartered cow as long as the milk supply continued abundant'. But the shape of things to come was as clear in Rhodesia as it had been in the Union: when in 1914 the Company's original twenty-five year term was running out the immigrants voted for extension, provided that independent government should be established as soon as the European population was large enough and the revenue sound enough.

A charmingly dated account of what part of Rhodesia was like before World War I exists in a book called, rather off-puttingly, *The Sunshine Settlers*, by Crosbie Garstin, written during the war. Mr Garstin begins by referring to rivers and railways. The rivers, 'just wide, deep channels of sand', held up the first motor-cars optimistically delivered—the wheels simply stuck, whirring uselessly; the railway, 'the Line of Least Resistance', brought slow, casual trains distributing goods and gossip along the single line linking Mafeking, Plumtree and Bulawayo. The settlers, 'a mixed lot', included 'younger sons kicked from the paternal door-step with a couple of thousand pounds, a first-class passage

An outskirt of Bulawayo, captured by the British forces (from a photograph by G. A. Phillips)

(single) and instructions to go to the devil somewhere out of sight', as well as many hopelessly beguiled by the Land Company's booklets that alluringly pictured

> the settler's rose-hung bungalow in the background (Mrs Settler entertaining a brace of fashionable duchesses to tea on the veranda), while the bearded settler himself sits astride his mettlesome Arab in the foreground and, with an upraised riding-whip, directs the harvesting of his crops.

But in reality wives were non-existent—'we of the veld lived for the most part alone, in pole and dab huts of our own construction, surrounded by troupes of Christy Minstrel retainers', cultivating the mealie and the ox, and keeping stores. One isolated storekeeper had as chef 'a nigger in spotless drill' who blew him to meals on a bugle. Mostly, however, the Matabele wore incongruous assortments of old clothes ('all the world's old clothes come to Africa'), and 'responded cheerfully to such names as "Cape Town", "Shilling", "Five", or "By m' by".' The settlers kept pets— cats, monkeys, baby fawns, chameleons, and, of course, dogs. They kept horses and mules. One day at the siding 'Messrs Begg and Wallace swung before our astonished gaze in a light Scotch-cart drawn by a four-in-hand of black donkeys ... A picanin, liveried in one of Begg's cast-off nightshirts, toppled off the tailboard, and stood to attention, tiger-wise, at the leaders' heads'. The donkeys, imported from the Free State, were to be used for everything, including playing polo. After one fiasco of a match, with an alarm-clock to signal the end of each chukka, donkeys were abandoned as sporting animals. The ox ('at his best, roast with horse-radish sauce') was slow and difficult, unlike the splendid spans of the south, taking hours to round up and inspan, and more hours to move a mile. The settlers were therefore thrown back upon horses, or the trains, which were all too apt to go 'dead lame, and then cast a wheel', leaving men stranded in some tiny town where the railway company's general factotum suggested that

> in two or three days the train would be coming back ... and if I would only mark time while he changed from a station-master into a civilian, he would show me the

sights, the bar, the town pump, the slaughter-poles, the mission church, introduce me to the local funny man, and do all he could to make my sojourn in their midst a memorable one.

Having 'read both sides of the Bulawayo Torch and Clarion', Mr Garstin 'spent two days in riotous living. On the third morning McAlpin sent a nigger to tell me that the train was in sight, and would be docked about noon'.

Mr Garstin camped out in the early days, enjoying the simplicity of lying in his camp bed under a mimosa-tree by a donga with two pools, one for bathing and one for drinking, the tree strung about with hat, coat, shaving-mirror, tins of food, buck-meat and a storm-lantern, until his nearest neighbour, Mr Page-Parsons, came along and criticized his primitive life: 'He said if I continued to live under a tree I would be up it ere long, cracking nuts'. When he built himself a house, he was plagued by white ants, which ate their way through everything, including bricks soaked in caustic soda. On a return visit, he found Mr Page-Parsons having a bath in a pool:

> 'You press the button and down comes the cold douche'. He jerked a pebble at a somnolent Makalaka, who woke up and emptied a bucket of slush over him.

Walking out one Sunday after the rains, wearing pink and white striped pyjamas and a sun-helmet, Mr Page-Parsons climbed a marula-tree to pick an orchid, leaving Mr Garstin at the bottom, but both charmed by the surrounding scenery:

> The scent of the yellow-powdered mimosas hung heavy and sweet on the air; scents of green springing things and warm wet earth arose like a soft steam all around; every furrow held a shining puddle, every dip a sky-mirroring pool. Clouds came foaming up from behind the Batanna Kops, and streamed across the blue like a fleet of white frigates making sail. All along the hill ridge, P-P's mealies stood green in the sun ... [Eventually] dusk came up green from the east, deepening into blue, spangled with a handful of white stars.

But the whole happy picnic was stopped dead in its tracks by the outbreak of the Kaiser's War.

> I got the news from the up-mail train not three hours ago; it went north burning the rails, everybody in the saloon drinking each other Good-bye. Old Pitcairn, the guard—who, it appears, won the DCM for smart arque-bus practice at Agincourt—dancing on a table, and challenging the Kaiser to a ten-round non-stop contest ... They've gone off home now to pack their tooth-brushes and oil their rifles, swearing to start an expedi-tion tomorrow to kill that Swiss storekeeper at Mazoi. Knox has nailed a cracker Union Jack to his veranda ... But, any way, his heart is in the right place; his gramophone plays Rule Britannia day and night, and ginger-pop is being stood gratis. Nevertheless, it is no laughing matter ...

It was not. The settlers went off to the war, where they were miserably homesick for their adopted country through-out.

Almost one-eighth of Rhodesia's total white population enlisted: the highest proportion of any British colonial terri-tory. The Union came in too, though by a slight margin, and Botha had to suppress a rebellion led by de Wet. There was always a strong Germanic leaning among the Afri-kaners, and perhaps it was appropriate that the Union was rewarded in 1919 by being given German South-West Africa as a mandated territory. This is an odd, remote, deserted place enormous and arid, with a few small towns scattered about. The capital, Windhoek, has three Rhine-style castles, and its main street is the Kaiserstrasse. One former German governor was the father of Hermann Goering. With this background it is easy to see why few British settled there, until, of course, the diamonds started to appear.

For parallel reasons, few British ever settled in Portuguese Mozambique, though British capital was widely invested there; nor have many British ever settled in the African states of Botswana, Lesotho, and Swaziland. These three lands, completely encircled by the Union, live in a state of nervous dependence upon the country they dislike but can-not manage without. Probably the best known British immi-grant is Ruth Williams, wife of Seretse Khama: when she married him he was one of the multitude of Africans in obscurity, exile or ignominy, but in 1965 he became Prime Minister of Bechuanaland and a year later, aged forty-five, first President of the Republic of Botswana. Miss Williams married him in 1948, and she could not then have had any idea that in less than twenty years she would be Lady Khama and first lady of her adopted country.

The leading Rhodesian of the twenties was Sir Charles Coghlan, who, though an Irish Catholic, was a man of Cromwellian looks and temperament, caring for neither the shareholders nor the Africans, but determined to protect the settlers' interests against both and against the idea of merging with the Union. He carried his battle to London in 1921, where he stood out against the Secretary of State, Winston Churchill, and back to Rhodesia, where a rowdy campaign led to the Referendum of 1922. On 26 October, the eve of poll, Coghlan's supporters broke up a pro-union meeting with heckling and rotten eggs; Lady Coghlan wrote: 'It was a grand night'; and Sir Charles said: 'The heart of Rhodesia beats soundly here in Bulawayo'. His party polled 8,774 votes to the opposition's 5,989.

The lowveld was nothing but raw scrub before World War I; after it a Scot, Tom MacDougall, began to clear a patch of it by hand. He bought a secondhand mill in Natal which took two years to reach him, travelling up by lorry and ox-wagon and crossing the border at Beit Bridge. By 1935 he produced ten tons of sugar, and today his firm has 20,000 acres in the great Triangle sugarlands of which he is the pioneer.

After 1919 it was, of course, never quite the same again. But Rhodesia remained unspoilt to an amazing degree for a number of years yet. Mrs Jasmine Rose Innes (married to a connexion of the great Sir James) was taken at the age of five from England to live at Rusape, midway between Salisbury and Umtali, where 'a little railway siding' with 'two Kaffir stores, corrugated iron hotel and police camp' was the focus of a few white farmers. Her father had gone out the year before under a grant scheme; the country was 'untouched, unfenced, almost unmapped' and had 'the cheapest labour in the world'—'black and white, the old status quo of master and servant which he understood'. Mrs Rose Innes was enchanted by ox-wagon travel, the endless hours of warm dreamy sunny progress, sitting on the plank seat in front or lying on the mattress spread over the floor of the cart, or walking barefoot in the 'silky dust' of the track. She loved the strange house they lived in, a 'cubicle of grass' with a springy cream-coloured cow-dung floor, renewed weekly, and the later, more orthodox house of home-made bricks that the family had to leave before they could pay for the windows. Her Rhodesia was empty, wild, beautiful, innocent and hardly touched, yet it was all so short a time ago.

Perhaps it was this quality that attracted Major Cecil Mercer to settle in Rhodesia after World War II. His highly popular books, published under his pen-name of Dornford Yates, dwell with sincere nostalgia on a world where the great English values still hold, where an ordered hierarchy of society defends its pounded bastions to the last. He chose the region of Umtali, and, on reading the guidebook, one is not surprised. The scenery is magnificent: mountains, cold glades, streams banked by flowers, sunlight flickering through tropical trees, surround the small, sleepy mountain town, containing such buildings as the Mountain Lodge Hotel (a thatched copy of an old English inn) and the Leopard Rock Hotel (designed like a picture-book castle, where African drummers announce mealtimes). To the creator of the 'English House' in Lisbon and the house that Berry Pleydell built in the Pyrenees among landscapes like these, Umtali appeared like paradise regained. His villains, never anything but full-blooded, would have been at home at the other end of the railway line, where the dockside night clubs of Lourenço Marques apparently sell a whisky that is 'liable to deprive you of speech for some days'; his heroes, ideal Pioneers, would have responded equally to the white-porticoed Government House on the site of Lobengula's royal kraal three miles out of Bulawayo, which has a model of the original kraal in a rondavel in the garden.

Another immigrant was Lord Graham, formerly the Duke of Montrose and to some the rightful king of Scotland, who left Eton for Oxford, took a degree in agriculture, and came to Rhodesia to farm. World War II did not stop him; he served in the Royal Navy, becoming a destroyer commander, and went back to become, later, Rhodesian Minister of Defence (indeed it is true that most of the men who have reached high office there have owned land). One of the most unusual was Godfrey Huggins, who came in 1911 when

Difficulties of travelling in South Africa: officers crossing the Ingagani River (from a contemporary sketch)

threatened with tuberculosis. He was already a qualified surgeon, and left a practice of £100 a year in London for one of £50 a month in Salisbury, where there were only four doctors at that time. He was of the pattern one learns to recognize: 'I wanted Africa to be a nice bright British pink, just as Rhodes did, all the way to Egypt.' In politics he never lost a seat and lived to be the last survivor of his own first Cabinet, having headed six ministries, but he maintained his interest and practical skill. To one angry caller he said: 'I know what is the matter with you, and I will be taking it out within six weeks'; it was the gall-bladder, and he did. Visited by a journalist, he asked all the questions, mostly on health, diagnosed appendicitis, and within an hour was operating on his surprised interviewer. A small man, with iron-grey hair and a neat moustache, lively brown eyes and an alert manner, he served on 17 February 1955 his 7,829th consecutive day as Prime Minister, a record unparalleled in the Commonwealth, and was finally raised to the Peerage as Lord Malvern. Another doctor achieving eminence in a different field is Dr Oliver Ransford, born in Bradford in 1914 and joining the British Colonial Medical Service in Nyasaland before World War II, during which he served in the RAMC; moving in 1947 to Bulawayo, where he still lives, he has made a considerable name for himself as a military historian, and his vivid, evocative accounts of Majuba Hill and Spion Kop are referred to elsewhere in these pages.

Home-born Britons were always socially at the top of the heap in Rhodesia, where nostalgic affection for a Britain most of them had never known pervaded every aspect of life. Treasured relics of English schools, regiments, clubs, and copies of *Country Life* and *The Tatler* revealed a loving preoccupation with an England that had virtually rejected them. Inadequately equipped to survive in Europe, they had the high status they wanted in Rhodesia. These were the mass of immigrants arriving between the wars. In the twenties it had been said: 'We are a third class people travelling first'. After World War II the pattern changed again. A new wave of Britons came out, finding the post-war government unbearable, but these had not the spiritual certainties of the earlier settlers, so that 'one of the last Rhodesian eccentrics, a sandalled scruffy son of a noble family, living in lonely squalor with his whisky and a fine library of books' told Mr

Frank Clements that 'Rhodesia is Surbiton in the bush'. Now matters have altered further still. Rhodesia is the only African settler country to produce its own accent, apart, of course, from the Union itself, and it is hard to exaggerate its importance in marking the real 'Ridgebacks' as a race apart. To hear the accent, if one finds it fascinating, one has only to listen to a speech by the present head of state, Mr Ian Smith.

Between the wars the Union strengthened its sympathies with Germany, to the point where Smuts carried the House in on the British side by only thirteen votes. The Afrikaner Nationalist Party never disguised its support for Hitler; in 1918 they set up at Potchefstroom what Mr Cope calls 'a powerful secret society with a gruesome initiation ritual' known as the Broederbond, conceived to promote Afrikaans and the trekboer ideals and dedicated to ruling the Union; 'its crowning achievement to date has been the providing of the Union with its four most recent Prime Ministers'.

Once the countries of Southern Africa were established as nations more or less in their own right, the whole question of immigration altered. No longer were people going to open up territories; they were going to places of clear-cut character like any others. Since 1910 British emigration to South Africa has tended more and more to be influenced by the controversial questions of opportunity and land versus Afrikaner nationalism; since 1966 the same trend has shown in Rhodesia. One interesting fact is that several contemporary poets are immigrants, such as Robert Dederick, born in 1919 and a solicitor by profession, who came to the Cape during the war and returned to settle there afterwards; Douglas Livingstone, born in 1932 and a bacteriologist, who served in the Rhodesian police before going to live in Durban; Mary Morison Webster, born in Edinburgh, emigrating with her family to Johannesburg in 1920; the late F. D. Sinclair, born in Scotland in 1921 and, like Dederick, coming to South Africa during the war (with the RAF) and settling after it in Pretoria.

The present-day emigrant to Southern Africa finds matters very different from what they were when the 1820 settlers scrambled ashore to open up the wilderness. Information in advance is showered upon him, details of housing facilities, employment prospects, taxation and licences, topics of interest to the housewife, education, climate and scenery, and assisted passages. One beautifully produced booklet quotes interviews with four families who went recently to live in four principal cities: Mr Gunther has described them as Cape Town, superbly set, with its 'golden, creamy atmosphere'; Johannesburg, sitting on gold; Durban, which 'looks like Brighton', region of Albert Luthuli and, originally, Mahatma Gandhi; and Port Elizabeth, which had no trees when Anthony Trollope visited it in 1878, based its economy on ostrich feathers and now makes cars, and has many monuments to Boer War British, 'including one to a horse'. The four interviews are scrupulous in weighing the comparisons between British and South African rents, prices, facilities, and conditions of work, stressing the need to work hard, and there seems no doubt that the ability to speak Afrikaans is crucial. The new immigrants like the climate, the schools, the opportunities for sport, and the fact that they can have servants. They like their detached, one-storey houses, and the comparative ease of motoring. They miss their relations, and they miss the English pub. Possibly the most startling difference, at least at first, is that there is no television in the Union. The British reader may well be struck by another omission: those interviewed do not seem aware of the history of their new country, nor of its exotic quality; their lives appear to follow the kind of pattern that shows in an English suburb.

The people who assist and advise immigrants call themselves The 1820 Settlers' Association, yet, of course, most of its members today are Afrikaner rather than British. Their advice includes the following :

> Do expect to find a country with horizons, clear skies, and good wide prospects for the energetic and imaginative, which is more concerned with what a man can do than the accent in which he describes it.
> Don't expect to find a land of milk and honey, to make a fortune overnight, to find that South Africa is a rather quaint survival of old colonial days. Don't express firm opinions about the country and people until you really know what you are talking about.

This is the closest the booklets come to suggesting that there is anything controversial in the Union today. The authors of books on Southern Africa, on the other hand,

invariably foresee trouble: the only point of variance among
them is when. All that one can truly say at this stage in this
sort of chronicle is that, looking at its history and the kind
of people who made it and whom it continues to fascinate
and to attract, the last word has not yet been heard from the
Cape of Storms.

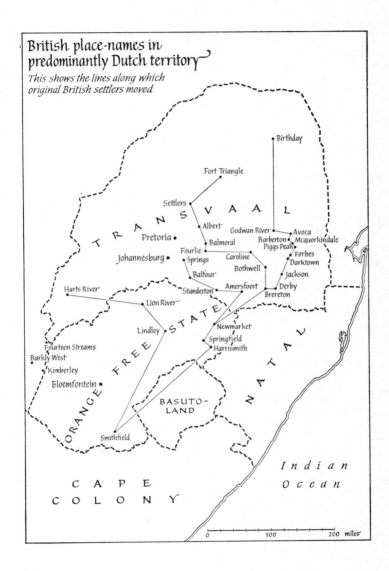

British place-names in predominantly Dutch territory

This shows the lines along which original British settlers moved

Birthday

Fort Triangle

Settlers

T R A N S V A A L

Albert

Pretoria

Godwan River · Avoca
Barberton · Mcquorkindale
Piggs Peak

Balmoral

Fourlie
Springs

Caroline

Forbes
Darktown

Johannesburg

Bothwell

Jackson

Balfour

Amersfoort

Derby
Brereton

Standerton

Harts River

Lion River

O R A N G E   F R E E   S T A T E

Newmarket

Lindley

Springfield
Harrismith

Fourteen Streams

Barkly West

N A T A L

Kimberley

Bloemfontein

BASUTO-
LAND

Smithfield

*Indian
Ocean*

C A P E
C O L O N Y

0   100   200 miles

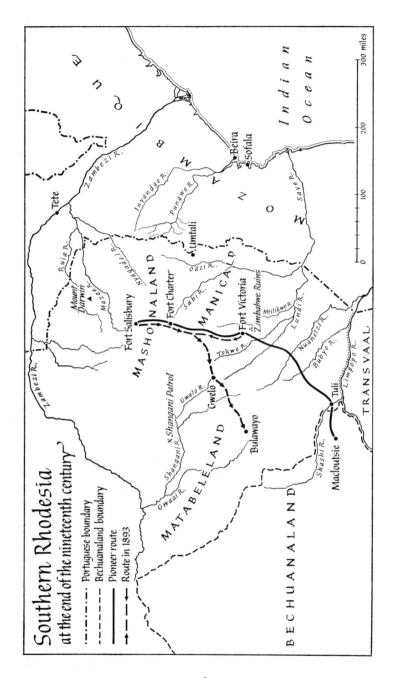

Southern Rhodesia
at the end of the nineteenth century

— · — Portuguese boundary
— — — Bechuanaland boundary
———— Pioneer route
— — → Route in 1893

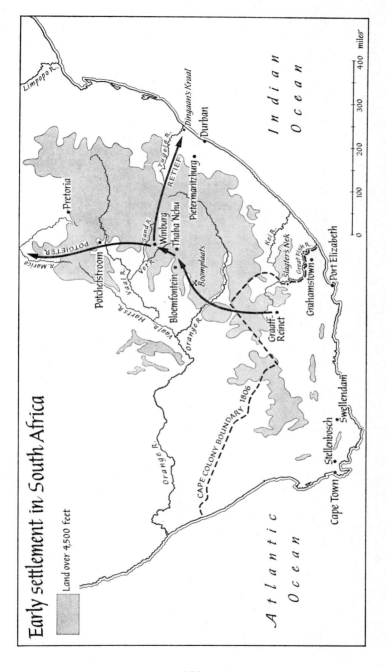

Early settlement in South Africa

Land over 4,500 feet

Southern Africa
in 1880

++++++ Railway

Belgian

Portuguese

R.Congo

L.Albert

L.Edward

L.Kivu

L.Rudolf

L.Victoria

L.Tanganyika

L.Mweru

Garenganze

Missions

L.Nyasa

Barotse

R.Zambezi

Mashona
Manica

Matabele

Portuguese

Walfish Bay

Bamangwato

R.Limpopo

Baralong

TRANSVAAL

R.Vaal

Delagoa Bay

R.Orange

ORANGE
FREE STATE

NATAL

Durban

CAPE COLONY

Cape Town

| 0 | 500 | 1000 | 1500 | 2000 miles |

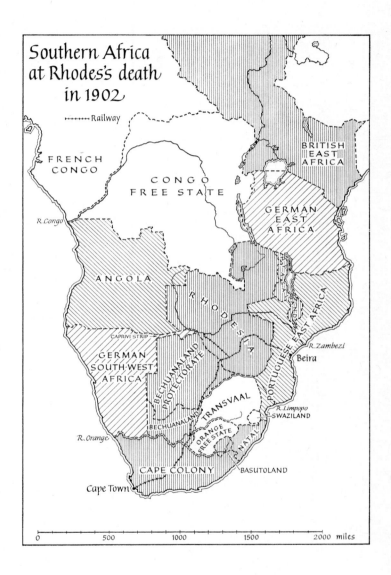

Southern Africa
at Rhodes's death
in 1902

········· Railway

FRENCH
CONGO

CONGO
FREE STATE

R. Congo

BRITISH
EAST
AFRICA

GERMAN
EAST
AFRICA

ANGOLA

R H O D E S I A

PORTUGUESE EAST AFRICA

CAPRIVI STRIP

GERMAN
SOUTH-WEST
AFRICA

BECHUANALAND
PROTECTORATE

R. Zambezi

Beira

BECHUANALAND

TRANSVAAL

R. Limpopo
SWAZILAND

R. Orange

ORANGE
FREE STATE

NATAL

CAPE COLONY

BASUTOLAND

Cape Town

0   500   1000   1500   2000 miles

111

Selected Bibliography

BOND, John, *They Were South Africans* (O.U.P., 1971)

BUCHAN, John, *Prester John* (Nelson, 1938)

BUNTING, Brian, *The Rise of the South African Reich* (Penguin, 1969)

CAMERON, James, *The African Revolution* (Thames & Hudson, 1961)

CARRINGTON, C. E., *The British Overseas: Exploits of a Nation of Shopkeepers: Vol. I, Making of the Empire* (C.U.P., 1968)

CHURCHILL, Winston S., *My Early Life* (Fontana, 1959)

CLEMENTS, Frank, *Rhodesia: The Course to Collision* (Pall Mall Press, London, 1969)

COPE, Jack, and KRIGE, Uys (eds.), *The Penguin Book of South African Verse* (1968)

COPE, John, *South Africa* (Benn, 1967)

DE KIEWIET, C. W., *A History of South Africa Social and Economic* (O.U.P., 1957)

EVANS, I. O., *The Observer Book of Flags* (Warne, 1959)

GANN, L. H., and DUIGNAN, P., *White Settlers in Tropical Africa* (Penguin, 1962)

GARDNER, Brian, *The Lion's Cage* (Arthur Barker, 1969)

GARDNER, Brian, *Mafeking* (Sphere Books, 1968)

GARSTIN, Crosbie, *The Sunshine Settlers* (Quality Press Ltd, 1943)

GUNTHER, John, *Inside Africa* (Hamish Hamilton, 1955)

HANNA, A. J., *The Story of the Rhodesias and Nyasaland* (Faber, 1960)

HEYER, Georgette, *The Spanish Bride* (Heinemann, 1952)

JACKSON, Stanley, *The Great Barnato* (Heinemann, 1970)

KEPPEL-JONES, Arthur, *South Africa: A Short History* (Hutchinson, 1966)

KRUGER, Rayne, *Goodbye Dolly Gray* (Four Square Books, 1964)

LOCKHART, J. G., and WOODHOUSE, C. M., *Rhodes* (Hodder & Stoughton, 1963)

MARQUARD, Leo, *The Story of South Africa* (Faber, 1970)

Selected Bibliography

MARTIN, Christopher, *The Boer War* (Abelard-Schuman, New York, 1969)

MAY Henry John, *Music of the Guns* (Jarrold, 1970)

MORRIS, Donald R., *The Washing of the Spears* (Cape, 1966)

PARKER, A. C., *The Springboks* (Cassell, 1970)

RANSFORD, Oliver, *The Great Trek* (John Murray, 1972)

RANSFORD, Oliver, *The Battle of Majuba Hill* (John Murray, 1968)

RANSFORD, Oliver, *The Battle of Spion Kop* (John Murray, 1969)

REED, Douglas, *Insanity Fair 1967: The Battle for Rhodesia* (Arthony Gibbs, 1967)

ROSE INNES, Jasmine, *Writing in the Dust* (André Deutsch, 1968)

SELBY, John, *The Boer War: A Study in Cowardice and Courage* (Arthur Barker, 1969)

SELBY, John, *Shaka's Heirs* (Allen & Unwin, 1971)

SHEPSTONE, Mrs S. W. B., *A History of Richmond, Natal, 1839–1937* (Durban, 1937)

SOUTH AFRICA IN THE SIXTIES: *A Socio-Economic Survey*, ed. H. T. Andrews, F. A. Berrill, Sir Francis de Guingand, Dr J. E. Holloway, Dr F. Meyer, Dr H. J. Van Eck (The South African Foundation, 1965)

TUCHMAN, Barbara W., *The Proud Tower* (Hamish Hamilton, 1966)

TRAVELLERS' GUIDE TO SOUTHERN AFRICA (Thornton Cox: Newman Neame, 1967)

Index

Index

116

Index

117

Index